"The difference between managers and leaders has widely been discussed. Rocking the Ship is for those who want to be leaders. I do not know any other business book providing more support and inspiration for those determined to define the future of their industries."

—Dr. HEIKO WOLTERS, Partner, Egon Zehnder

"Rocking the Ship brings business innovation to a new level. Its Business Model Radar combines core elements of Kim's and Mauborgne's Strategy Canvas and Osterwalder's Business Model Canvas. It follows the Design Thinking philosophy, and the Nightmare Competitor approach provides an intriguing twist. Hats off to Uli and Mat!"

—OLIVER SCHMID, Executive Director, frog design

"A very well-structured approach to a difficult topic: how to reinvent your business model. It inspires you to think about setting priorities, how to change your business model, and your responsibilities as a leader.?"

—ISABEL DIAZ ROHR, Executive Board Member, BENTELER International AG

"We use the Nightmare Competitor approach to create disruptive business models in fast-changing markets. If you want to rock your ship, it's the only tool that shows you clearly what will happen if an aggressive competitor enters with new ideas."

—PETER GERSTMANN, President & CEO, Zeppelin GmbH

"A must-read for anyone captive in an organization or industry awaiting its inevitable disruption. It is fair to say that nobody has thought longer, harder, or smarter about the innovation immunity of corporations and how to overcome it. One of the best business books of (at least) the year—and a very different one."

—SEBASTIAN WOHLRAPP, CEO, CINTEO

"Uli and Mat are the nightmare competitors of the consulting industry. With Rocking the Ship, they enable managers and top executives to achieve astonishing results in almost no time. Far better than spending lots of money only to end up with the usual 'not invented here' objections. Great guys to work with. Together with our clients, we are delighted."

—JOCHEN GEIS, CEO, Zürich International Business School (ZIBS)

"Grothe's and Lock's book addresses one of the most important issues in strategy development for any business: creating new business models and foreseeing possible attacks by new emerging competitors. The methods presented are very practical and of high value for anybody innovating future business."

—DR. STEFAN GIRSCHIK, Deputy CEO, Rehau Group

"Rocking the Ship is the most relevant and progressive business book I have read in a very long time. The content is mapped into real-life examples and offers a straightforward, no-nonsense approach for those in business who understand the need to think and act like start-ups. It's a must-read for any manager, business owner, or entrepreneur who needs to analyze competitors and disrupt operating markets for their business's growth and survival."

—STEPHEN PASCALL, Director, Management.Commercial.Engineering

"This approach is fresh and new; it's very different from the traditional tools we use. I appreciated not relying on specific business experts. In our case, we invited all departments and let them bring their brains into it."

—ALEXANDER GERFER, CTO, Würth Elektronik eiSos Gruppe

"As a psychologist, I say, chapeau! Leading managers to virtually and playfully attack their own business offers totally new insights. Such insights are crucial for transforming companies. This book offers an inspiring, mind-blowing experience, enabling you to move on to new business dimensions with courage and creativity."

—DR. JANA LEIDENFROST, Coach and Author

"Not all approaches to business innovation work well in Asian cultures. However, to simulate how an outsider would attack your industry is universally applicable, and this book provides a uniquely simple and systematic means to doing just that."

—WOLFGANG BIERER, CEO, ENDEAVOR SBC

"An entertaining and inspiring reading for anybody dealing with strategy and business transformation, if you are really ready to question the status quo! This book provides a very helpful framework to structure necessary paranoia into actionable insight."

—MARK THOMÄ, SVP Marketing & Sales, DEKRA SE

"To come up with business innovations for the health sector, especially for hospitals, is extremely challenging. The industry is heavily regulated, lots of shareholders need to be managed, and the well-being of patients can never be compromised. We gave employees of all ranks and functions the chance to define their future, and a two-day Rocking the Ship workshop was all it took. We are amazed and thrilled."

—MARKUS MORD, CEO, Vinzenz von Paul Hospitals

"Successful leaders have the ability to challenge themselves and their business environment. They have vision, courage, empathy, and are able to initiate change. This book provides you with numerous opportunities to (re-)calibrate your current way of leading in all of these aspects. The Rocking the Ship workshop fascinated and encouraged me. I can only recommend that you give it a try—it works!"

—ALEXANDER D'HUC, Managing Director, DLL India

"Digital technology and new business models are changing the world. Rocking the Ship provides me with a framework to combine these two drivers. The methodology and examples offered help enormously to make sure we do not compromise."

—ERIK VON GÖLER, Director, Digital BITZER

"For me the Corporate Spaceship story created much-needed and sobering clarity. As corporate managers, we need to continually challenge the traditional thinking that has allowed our organizations to become outdated. Rocking the Ship provides inspiring and tangible ways to do that."

—KURT DEPPERT-LATTKI, SVP Business Development,
TÜV SÜD Auto Service Division

"Having worked with both Ulrich and Mat on numerous strategic and innovation projects, I greatly enjoyed and appreciated both their energy and their tireless passion to approach business in a very different way. They encourage people around them to break free from conventional beliefs and adopt an open mind as a critical step toward customer-centric business growth."

—HOLGER KLEIN, Managing Director, Dräger Japan

Rocking the Ship

ROCKING THE SHIP

Turning corporate managers into
business model mavericks

ULI GROTHE & MAT LOCK

Rocking the Ship

©2017 Uli Grothe & Mat Lock

This book was designed by THE FRONTISPIECE. The text face is Mercury Text, first designed by Jonathan Hoefler and Tobias Frere-Jones in 1997, with other elements set in Eurostile LT Std.

ISBN PRINT 978-1-61961-809-1
ISBN EBOOK 978-1-61961-810-7

LIONCREST
PUBLISHING

TABLE OF CONTENTS

DEAR FELLOW MANAGERS,

You are the ones who can change the world into an even more exciting place. A place where people are eager to explore the new and to create great things every day.

We all know that the corporate world does not live up to this aspiration as well as it could. This is not satisfying for anybody.

We are setting out to rock the ships of the corporate world. And they will be rocked when you become Business Model Mavericks.

Interested in rocking your corporation? Then this book is for you.

INTRODUCTION

Over the past few centuries, established companies have been the main growth driver in many economies. They seem incapable, however, of developing groundbreaking new business models to secure a future for themselves in a rapidly changing world.

It was not the established automotive industry that paved the way for electro-mobility; it was Tesla. Neither carmakers nor public transport companies have kick-started the debate around revolutionary new forms of urban mobility; it was Google with its self-driving car project. The established coffee companies were incapable of reinventing their industry; Starbucks had to do the job. The mobile phone companies never provided their customers with a universe of applications; it needed Apple. The hotel industry never took into consideration that customers might appreciate living in others' apartments until Airbnb came along. Camera companies were only interested in improving their products and left it up to Instagram to show what can be done with images.

Banking, insurance, food, energy utility, legal, medical, agriculture, consulting, IT, retail, and so on. It is damned hard to find exceptions. Huge marketing and R&D efforts do not make the difference, and cohorts of consultants seem to miss the mark. Valuable assets and expertise that could be used to reinvent the future of industries are wasted. We cannot and should not accept this. Managers of established organizations need to become better at business innovation. They owe it to their customers, their employees, their shareholders, and themselves.

The established can become better. To do so, they must go back to where they once began, when they were the newcomers themselves. Startups and industry outsiders are apparently creating groundbreaking business innovations with great ease. Their lifeblood is thinking the other way around. Fighting conventional wisdom is their creed.

Almost all the established had this capability in the beginning. We hear managers say, "In our early days, we were once like the ones who are attacking us today." And these managers tell us how they worked their butts off, thriving on success. They remember the fire in the eyes of their teams and how enthusiastic customers were. But we also hear them complain, "This is no longer the company I used to work for."

Managers need to become Business Model Mavericks again! This book is for all those who are not ready to settle into golden cages, and do not want to pray that the given system will last until retirement. Instead, it is for all managers and employees of organizations, regardless of function, rank, or industry, who know deep down that failing to make use of the huge potential lying in our organizations and employees is a massive oversight. Think of this as a handbook for breaking free from convention.

Our priority isn't to please academia. The game of quoting as many other authors as possible for the sake of raising academic status does not really create value. Empirical analyses carried out over several months or years run the danger of being outdated even before going to print. We didn't apply for our texts to be edited by the presumed authorities in the field. Bear in mind that thus far, the academic system could not provide a generally accepted framework for established organizations to succeed in inventing and launching groundbreaking new business models. We aspire to be bolder and faster.

We describe our approach for rocking the ships of the corporate world in five short chapters.

The first chapter, "Corporate Spaceships," describes the metamorphosis from startup to established. Even though no company aspires to turn from the youthful, brave, and innovative startup into a greyed, self-centered, and rather immobile member of the established, it seems inevitable. The first step to deal with this involuntary transformation is to become aware of the forces driving it. You'll understand why the established are doomed to grow as soon as innovation begins to fade. It will become apparent why the strategies and specialists employed to foster growth, the systems built to harness the expansion, and the networks they've created interfere with their ability to adapt.

The vulnerability of the incumbents allows startups and industry outsiders to turn whole industries upside down. Technological innovation is not the fundamental growth engine of the attackers. Newcomers strike with a weapon the incumbents have never learned to master. They win by introducing new business models. In a worst-case scenario, newcomers design such models in a way that the incumbent's assets become liabilities and their strengths turn into weaknesses. In this way, the intruders establish new rules for the game. And as soon as these rules find acceptance, the established have no choice but to comply. In the second chapter, "Nightmare Competitors," we'll familiarize you with the strategies of such attackers.

You will see that you can free yourself from self-centered planning routines by looking at the world from the odd perspective of such Nightmare Competitors. And when the focus of the exercise moves from understanding the power of Nightmare Competitors to creating *virtual* Nightmare Competitors, you're already embarking on a journey that will lead you far into the realm of previously unconsidered business opportunities. We show that it's possible to create new business models systematically and that the process is exciting.

Once you're able to understand existing Nightmare Competitors better and create virtual Nightmare Competitors, the time is right to move to the next chapter. Most industries are in danger of being attacked simultaneously from different angles. The attacking Nightmare Competitors, real or virtual, are usually seen as niche players. They don't reach the threshold in which the incumbent's alarm bells start to ring. However, the loss of even a few percentage points of market share here and a few there can easily add up to significant numbers. And in most industries, a loss of 10 percent in sales is the difference between highly profitable and being ankles-deep in the mud.

When managers are fully aware of the consequences of multiple potential attacks, they acquire "Intellectual Leadership." In the third chapter of our book, you'll learn to differentiate various types of attackers. It will quickly become apparent that these attackers are much more customer-centric than the established companies in their present setup. In this respect, your organization might be vulnerable, too. You'll find out about and be able to attain Intellectual Leadership in your industry while going through this chapter.

The Intellectual Leadership of an elite group of senior managers isn't sufficient. For "Rocking the Ship," large parts of the whole organization need to be engaged. In Chapter 4, we describe how great numbers of managers can become Business Model Mavericks. We'll also familiarize you with the Mavericks Matrix. This tool helps you make sure you are not compromising too early. The Mavericks Matrix also allows you to convince supervisory boards and shareholders that slowing down initiatives or watering down new approaches is not an option.

There is a high chance that at the end of this process, everyone involved will commit to the creed, "We won't allow anybody else to determine the future of our industry. We are going to take care of this ourselves." Then, the gleam returns to the eyes of formerly frustrated managers. If you aspire to harnessing this power, Chapter 4 is for you.

Usually, there's a demand for new approaches, as well as the current ones. We are moving further and further away from a world where "one size fits all" thinking is adequate. So, it isn't about changing the strategy of a whole organization or substituting one activity for another. It's about being able to provide surroundings in which diverse, even competing business models can prosper. In Chapter 5, "Keep on Rocking," we describe how flexible spacecrafts can be launched alongside traditional spaceships.

We will discuss concepts that give customers and employees the chance to choose. In this new world, the traditional concepts for strategic planning and change are not really applicable anymore. The corporate ship is ultimately rocked when established business entities are willing to supply new entities with input that no Nightmare Competitors can get hold of. Then, it is possible to surpass even the most nightmarish ones. We conclude this book by describing how this is done.

Our book is full of case studies. They cover various industries in both business-to-consumer (B2C), as well as business-to-business (B2B) industries. However, one industry serves as a lead example: the automotive industry. Almost every reader owns a car. Even those who don't are familiar enough with the industry. It's an industry that is simply too important to be overlooked. And it's an industry in turmoil. It would be foolish not to make use of these perfect preconditions.

This book represents the journey of two guys who refuse to watch from the sidelines. Instead, we aspire to empower members of organizations to gain control and become the authors of their own destiny. This book is a testimony to what we, Uli Grothe and Mat Lock, have achieved so far. We're still as thrilled as we were on the day we set off, and we are looking forward to continuing the journey.

If you share our aspiration, please join us. To connect with us on social media or access bonus templates and tutorial videos, please visit our website at:

www.rockingtheship.com/bookresources

①

CORPORATE
SPACESHIPS

When Carl Benz rode to university on his bicycle, he was often deep in thought. The adaptation of steam engines to rotary motion brought an end to the era of sailing ships and was one of the driving forces behind the industrial revolution, as steam-driven trains were able to transport goods and people more cost-effectively over long distances.

The horse-driven carriages he saw everywhere seemed antiquated to him. These thoughts never left him; not during his studies nor when he started his professional career. He was a stubborn character and didn't fit well in any of the companies he worked for. He founded his own company while being supported by his wife. After encountering several hardships, he finally made it. In 1885, Carl Benz created the first horseless carriage, the automobile. It featured wire wheels like the ones on his bicycle. The four-stroke engine he had designed was placed between the rear wheels. The engine had a coil ignition and evaporative cooling. Two roller chains transmitted the power of the engine to the rear axle. On the 29th of January 1886, he received a patent for his motorcar.

Benz began selling his motorcar in the late summer of 1888, making it the first commercially available automobile in history. His second customer was Parisian bicycle manufacturer, Emile Roger, who had already been building Benz engines under license from Carl Benz for several years. Roger added the Benz automobiles to the line he carried in Paris. Of the few cars sold at this early stage, most were sold there. From today's perspective, it is hard to imagine that the early 1888 version of the motorcar still had no gears and could not climb hills unaided.

An important part of the Benz story was its first long-distance trip by his equally entrepreneurial wife, Bertha Benz. The idea was a stroke of marketing genius, intended to demonstrate the feasibility of using the Benz motorcar for extended travel. Her husband was unaware that she planned to take their vehicle on a 106-km (sixty-six-mile) trip to visit her mother with their children. It was an arduous journey that involved various challenges and led to some groundbreaking innovation. There were multiple technical issues requiring attention. Fueling up meant locating pharmacies along the route. She had a shoemaker nail leather padding onto the brakes after traversing some long downhill sections. Bertha and the children finally arrived at nightfall and announced their success to Carl by telegram.

The car was introduced to the world at the 1889 World's Fair in Paris. The company producing the vehicles, Benz & Cie, grew from fifty employees in 1889 to 430 in 1899. During the final years of the nineteenth century, Benz was the largest automobile company in the world with 572 units produced in 1899.

The leadership of Benz & Cie was first challenged by the Daimler Motor Company. Many other players then entered the scene, turning the automobile into a worldwide phenomenon. In the 1890s, there were hundreds of manufacturers. For many decades, the United States led the world in total automobile production. Crises, however, had an impact. The German economic crisis led Daimler Motoren Gesellschaft and Benz & Cie to cooperate. But even such severe crises did not have an impact on the overall development of the industry. The automotive industry became one of the most important industries worldwide.

Comparable stories about other great inventors and how their inventions led to the evolution of whole industries can easily be told. Alessandro Volta, who invented the battery, can be used as an example. Samuel Colt, inventor of the revolver, might be the favorite example for those who carry guns. Samuel Morse, the inventor of the telegraph and Alexander Graham Bell, the inventor of the telephone are certainly worth mentioning. Thomas Alva Edison, who illuminated the world with his light bulb, was a genius of rank. Or there's the Wright Brothers, who taught the world to fly. Henry Ford developed the great idea to build complicated products on assembly lines. Gregory Pincus's invention, the contraceptive pill provided the basis for the sexual revolution. As people who love to write, we praise Ladislao Biro for inventing his ballpoint pen. But, as authors, we wonder whether we would've enjoyed writing this book as much without Henry Roberts's invention, the PC. The potential list of inventors and the industries that evolved out of their amazing achievements is endless.

The problem, however, is that such stories can't be conveyed as never-ending tales of successes and achievements. Many of the pathfinders did well for a long time, but started to struggle at a certain point. Numerous players that devoted themselves to enriching the world by making something new have since lost steam. Despite well-known meta-trends, the automotive industry has not managed to come up with convincing green solutions or concepts that help deal with traffic congestion. Despite all warnings, the financial industry created a severe crisis by launching dubious artificial investment products, yet they keep on placing such problematic offerings. Similarly, the health industry struggles to remember the oath of Hippocrates and raw material and oil and gas companies are exploiting the planet like there's no tomorrow.

Most industries do not stay true to the ingenious spirit of those who provided the basis for their existence. And neither trying harder nor doing more of the same, appear to be the right directive. How can the lack of creativity and "fresh energy" of whole industries be explained? By applying a certain level of abstraction, an interesting pattern becomes apparent.

It all begins with an invention. A new product or service offers the chance to provide unprecedented value for customers. However, just as Carl Benz's car was imperfect at the outset, so too are most inventions. From the viewpoint of the inventors, customers willing to pay for and make use of their inventions are almost as far away as distant planets.

If customers are remote planets, a company is the spaceship created to reach them. It consists of some form of production, no matter how rudimentary. Sales and marketing need to be taken care of. Logistical aspects require attention. Invoicing, bookkeeping, and other administrative tasks are also in demand for this spaceship to function. Without employees, none of this can be managed. Therefore, the spaceship is manned with a crew.

Of course, there's the question of which planets to travel to and, respectively, which customers should be served first.

Planets that are relatively easy to reach and do not require the most sophisticated of spaceships are naturally chosen. Delivering a proof of concept is more important than perfecting it. Things inevitably go wrong, and hardships must be endured. But after lessons have been learned the hard way, the first planet is successfully reached.

After that, comparable planets are chosen and a certain stability of processes and a level of product quality can be established. People begin to see the potential of traveling to the planets, and they regard the spaceship as sufficiently trustworthy and reliable. Some apply for jobs and bring valuable competencies; others are willing to provide money. On this basis, tremendous progress is made. There's no doubt the spaceship has connected the invention with customers. Thanks to the company, a substantial number of customers benefit from the invention.

More and more planets are reached, meaning more and more customers are able to be addressed. The voyages become lucrative. The story about the inventor, the remarkable invention, and the spaceship which made it accessible, spread around the world. The name of the spaceship, that is, the name of the company becomes synonymous for that which is new. This commercial success allows further investments. They make expansions of the activities possible. The spaceship grows in size and becomes a corporate spaceship.

Others see the riches that can be earned with corporate spaceships and jump onto the bandwagon. They start to build spaceships, too. There is no need to reinvent the wheel. Therefore, their corporate spaceships greatly resemble the original. This is the way the first competitors enter the scene.

After the relatively "easy-to-reach" planets have been explored by numerous spaceships, the novelty starts to fade off. To compensate for this, the basic invention is constantly improved. New releases are brought to the market at regular intervals, and more capable spaceships are built. These corporate spaceships enable them to reach planets no one has traveled to before. Specialists for expansion are hired. Research and development takes care of the new releases. The marketing department is assigned with the task of identifying uncharted planets. These efforts combined make it possible to land on planets with even the most challenging climatic and topographical conditions. A byproduct, however, is that the corporate spaceships now resemble gigantic multifunctional machines.

The competition between the corporate spaceships naturally become an arms race. Each crew claims they've achieved more and that they're better than the others. But the reality is that all of them are highly capable. Each move of rivaling corporate spaceships is monitored closely. Insight gained out of competitive intelligence efforts are then used to challenge each of their own efforts. As a consequence, the spaceships become look-alikes. From a distance, it's almost impossible to tell them apart.

Because differentiation is increasingly difficult, a hunt begins for economies of scales. They allow efficiency gains, and by now, these gains appear to be the greater lever for increasing or at least maintaining profitability. Departments are formed to identify and exploit synergies. Each of these efficiency-focused departments is staffed with functional specialists who define standards and procedures with which everybody on the corporate spaceships has to comply. There is no longer room for experimenting. Only suggestions likely to pay off within a short timespan are given the green light. Everything has to follow a predefined plan. And the personal performance of the spaceship crew must meet clearly defined objectives.

Subsequently, economies of scale become the Holy Grail. Better utilization of the corporate spaceships allows the business to cover investments faster. Further economies of scale can be achieved by running as many spaceships as possible. Mergers and acquisitions are carried out to allow for even greater scaling. Industry consolidation sets in.

Pursuing expansion- and efficiency-oriented strategies at the same time, however, has consequences. Expansion requires *diverse* approaches. Efficiency calls for *standardization*. So, compromises need to be made. The internal debates consume enormous amounts of time. Because of the ubiquitous "forced party truces," nobody is genuinely happy. Power play sets in. The enthusiasm that once unified the crew and was the basis for great accomplishments is long gone. The universe outside the spaceship is no longer the challenge; instead, it's the microcosms within the ships.

By this point, it's almost impossible to maneuver these huge spaceships. The complexity of technology, processes, and social interactions is overburdening. And, there's always the chance that even the smallest change could have enormous unforeseeable ripple effects. If there is no absolute necessity, nobody dares to change the running system.

Unfortunately, the whole process is self-enforcing. Every stakeholder, from employee to supplier, is benefiting from it. Why should they have an interest in changing anything? Nobody has any motivation to stand up and say, "Hold on, let's think about it. It can't go on like this."

Of course, there are consultants out there. However, most of them are specialists in expansion or efficiency strategies. And there are malicious tongues claiming they're actually one of the driving forces behind the obvious convergence. It's said that all their white papers and benchmarking reports are part of the problem, rather than being part of the solution. Every corporate spaceship has access to the same studies. Therefore, they all base their decisions on similar assumptions.

Finally, associations are founded and funded by all corporate spaceships to lobby their interests. These associations might ask for concessions to travel to planets that had been legally off-limits, for subsidies or tax reductions. And to be granted these privileges, associations never tire to recite the mantra of how important the spaceships of their industry are for the well-being of national economies and employment.

The reality is, the creators of the system do not have the system under control any longer. Over time and generations of managers, a system evolved that unnoticeably gained control over them.

We assume you've already considered whether our corporate spaceship metaphor is representative of the way your own company evolved and is now "part of an industry." It's usually no problem for people to make the link. However, *where* people connect with our story differs, of course. Some companies started as inventors, others as copycats, some are still doing well, and nobody has started to worry. Other companies are in the process of losing control or are already governed by their "out of control" systems. People working within the latter type of organizations often describe themselves as being "corporate captives." No matter how high they've made it within the hierarchy of their organizations, they feel constrained by multiple shackles.

The analogy of the corporate spaceship might help you avoid getting stuck in corporation-specific details. The high level of abstraction or the high-flight level allows you to see how vulnerable most companies and, in fact, most industries are. These immobile giants are easy prey for intelligent attackers.

②

NIGHTMARE COMPETITORS

Goliath was six feet nine inches tall. He was the strongest soldier in the Philistine army. He was not impressed when he saw who the Israelites sent to fight him. We all know how the story ended: David was well aware of the giant's weaknesses and changed the rules of the game. With a simple sling, he slew his opponent and became the victor of the battle of Elah. Mighty Achilles was killed by the weakling Paris. Like David, Paris knew about the vulnerability of his opponent.

Both stories are merely two of the most prominent of thousands of stories describing that the presumably strong can be overcome by those perceived as weak. The business world is full of such examples. We call the Davids and the

Parises of the business world, "Nightmare Competitors," because like them, they don't accept rules and win by exerting their very own strategies.

Knowing the weapons favored by the established is crucial in this context. And the Nightmare Competitors are well aware that technological innovation is the weapon of choice of the established. As described in the spaceship story of Chapter 1, it is the basis of their existence. Excelling via technology is in their muscle memory. But their reliance on technological innovation is not only their strength, but their weakness, as well.

The established are the least prepared and the most vulnerable when they are attacked with a totally different weapon—a divergent business model. Tesla and the industry serving as our lead example, the automotive industry, are perfect for illustrating how business-model innovation can turn the world of those who rely predominantly on technological innovation upside down.

Tesla was founded in 2003 by somebody you'd hardly call an inventor in the traditional sense. Elon Musk is, rather, a serial entrepreneur stirring up one industry after another by implementing new business models. Tesla relied heavily on readily available technologies just like PayPal, SolarCity, and SpaceX, some of his other ventures. Electric vehicles were invented even before anyone dreamed of combustion engines. And bundling lithium ion batteries out of laptops to extend capacity does not really qualify as a fundamental technological innovation, at least not as an innovation the incumbents would have been incapable of developing.

Tesla is leading the world into the age of electro-mobility. And let's be clear, they did it without subsidies or tax incentives. Such incentives are certainly great if you can get them. However, they were never a prerequisite for Musk. Tesla made its way in a time when the mighty carmakers around the globe said the transformation would require joint approaches and substantial governmental support.

And Tesla made its way in times when some carmakers saw their future in creatively optimizing diesel engines. Sales of the Tesla Model S in the United States in 2016 were nearly double those of the closest contender, the Mercedes-Benz S-Class, and more than double those of the BMW 7 Series. Altogether, the Model S actually accounted for nearly one-third of the total large luxury sedan market in the U.S. It took the incumbents more than a decade to take Tesla seriously. But now, all of them are trying to follow the innovator. Following a newcomer definitely has nothing to do with strategic leadership.

The easiest way to find out how Tesla is turning the assets of the incumbents into liabilities, and their perceived strengths into weaknesses, is to look at the story from their side. Therefore, we need to go back to 2003, when Tesla started to think about how they could make electro-mobility successful.

So, let's assume we're looking over the shoulders of

Elon Musk and his team members. Like every would-be Nightmare Competitor, the Tesla team is challenging each and every thing the incumbents are proud of. Every time they stumble upon something that could be seen as an industry imperative, they ask whether it's still adequate, whether the same objective could be achieved with another approach, and so on. There is nothing they're ready to accept as holy.

The established carmakers are proud of their range of models. From sports cars to sedans to SUVs to convertibles, coupes, vans, and minivans, they offer a vehicle for every purpose. Every niche is covered. The range goes from small to large and from basic to luxurious. In the case of BMW, there's a range from Mini to 1 series up to 7 series and even Rolls Royce. Mercedes has a range from the Smart cars to the Maybach. And all brands are offering super-premium sports vehicles. Therefore, they have special entities like the M division of BMW, Mercedes' AMG or the Quattro division of Audi. Does a newcomer really need this complexity? They could start with a very limited range. For the narrow target audience of a newcomer, this should be sufficient. There is no need to make everybody happy.

The automotive industry is also proud of all the features and engine concepts it's offering. In part, these options are required due to the range of models. Small city cars need different configurations than sports cars. And by providing options, the carmakers allow customers to tailor their cars to their preferences. This ensures that every customer can find what they are looking for. A newcomer would not need this second layer of complexity, either. The outsider only needs to provide the options relevant for their type of cars. In this sense, it would be ideal to offer just one type of engine concept. And there is an upside to such self-imposed limitations. The brand of the Nightmare Competitors would stand out. It would simply not be a car for everybody. Excellent! The product would become desirable because it is exclusive.

The next thing that's seen as a great asset by all the incumbents are their dealerships. All of them have established nationwide networks of independent representatives. The dealers are actually the real customers of the car manufacturers. They buy the cars and promote them afterward to end users. This is a convenience for the established car companies, as someone else is investing in outlets, cars, sales representatives, and mechanics.

But what are the downsides of having dealerships? First, it's difficult for the manufacturers to sell cars directly to end users. Car dealers demand to be the exclusive sales channel and expect a handsome margin for the cars they sell. After all, they invest heavily in representing the car manufacturers' brand. However, exclusivity is problematic when purchasing a car on the Internet becomes a viable option for more and more customers, especially when they're not overwhelmed with a multitude of options. Second, the dealerships suspect, of course, that the carmakers would like to introduce such direct sales through the back door. Therefore, they're reluctant to share customer data with the manufacturers. A newcomer would never ever want to rely on middlemen dealers; as an attacker, they'd want to talk directly to the customer. They would opt for online sales wherever possible and provide physical touch points where their customers are likely to be, i.e., shopping malls and city centers.

In the traditional system, dealerships are not only needed for sales but also for servicing cars. The servicing business has been of great importance to the relationship between carmaker and dealer. The manufacturers reduced the margins for selling cars by allowing the dealers to earn handsome profits when servicing cars. The dealers are eager to sell cars to get access to as much servicing work as possible. But how much service is needed if you would be selling cars with electric motors rather than combustion engines? There's hardly anything that can wear out or requires adjustment. And such an attacker would be well aware that the "money-making machine" the established have created at the customer's expense provides a nice story for the media.

But what if a car really needs servicing? Since there would be no dealer to interfere, many problems could be fixed directly via remote software updates. It might be feasible to even establish a pick-up service and the provision of a spare car if a vehicle needs to be brought in for maintenance. In a 180-degree reversal of the status quo, the company would come to see the client when there is a problem. For a smaller player, this would probably be a more efficient solution anyway.

If it's not just about selling technology but, rather, about providing a new system, how about establishing a network of chargers accessible only for cars of the attacker's brand? In the beginning, the charging could even be free. How about connecting the charging with private green energy generation? Industry boundaries would be crossed. But wasn't it the intention right from the start to jump out of the box? For the established, this would provide another obstacle. And there is a limit to the number of obstacles they can overcome simultaneously.

The economies of scale which the established can rely on are hard to beat. When it comes to purchasing costs, automating processes, and spreading the immense cost for R&D and other functions, they possess an enormous strength. What could be done about this? The most important and expensive ingredient when it comes to electro-mobility is the battery. Wouldn't it be possible to build up economies of scales there? With a focus on electro-mobility, the attackers could end up with higher volumes of batteries than the mixed fleets of the established and, therefore, radically drive down the cost of batteries.

The newcomers could already dream of a gigantic battery factory. And the factory could be utilized by introducing more electric models. Based on the economies of scale in the battery sector, the newcomer could even profitably sell mass-market models. There would even be another way to utilize the factory: powerful batteries could also be used to make homes and factories less dependent on electrical grids. With such batteries, they could buffer energy they create via solar panels or wind turbines and become self-sustainable. Furthermore, the attacker could allow other automakers to make use of their cost advantages. Some car manufacturers might then source the batteries from the attacker. The weaker manufacturers, especially, would most likely struggle to resist the temptation.

The company could then feed the press with all the elements already discussed. With such a radical approach, the newcomer would definitely be the darling of the media, especially the business-oriented. Readers, many of whom could be buyers, would be instrumental in spreading the news. It goes without saying that the media would question the integrity of the established. After all, how consistent is it to sell green cars and gas-guzzling monsters at the same time?

Taking all of this into account, traditional marketing would hardly be required. All the money spent on campaigns, sponsorship, motorsports, and VIP programs could be repurposed to establish, for example, an infrastructure for electric charging. The world would soon be divided into enthusiasts and skeptics. And enthusiasts often team up to form clubs, help each other out, and are ready to make the concession always required when new approaches are introduced. Couldn't the attackers start small to minimize the risk? Maybe an extreme sports car would be good to begin with. Such a car could demonstrate the sensation of the incredible acceleration that electric engines are capable of. Electromobility would actually be exciting, not merely rational and boring, as with the early electric cars of the incumbents. The lighter weight of a sports car would also allow reasonable travel ranges. Besides, nobody wants to travel long distances in an extreme sports car anyway. So, range really would not be a problem. And in an expensive sports car, the relatively high cost of the battery could easily be hidden.

After having learned a lot with relatively small effort, a real car could be brought to the markets. In Europe, it could be introduced first in countries like Switzerland or Norway, where people and governments are very environmentally conscious, purchasing power is a given, and strict speed limits would ensure that the range is indeed close to what can be reached under ideal circumstances.

Following a process like this, the still comparatively small David from California became the Nightmare Competitor of the incumbents and is now determining the strategy of the Goliaths around the globe.

How valuable would it have been for the established to see the potential of Tesla's approach early on? They could have occupied the position Tesla is now holding by developing their own similarly innovative business models.

Can such business models be created systematically at an early stage and by almost anyone? Our answer is an enthusiastic, "Yes!" In the following chapters, we'll familiarize you with the methodology that allows you to do exactly that.

BUSINESS MODEL CONSTITUENTS

To create business models systematically, it is important to be aware that both types of companies, the established and the attackers, have business models. It may be that the established are struggling to alter their business model as we have discussed in Chapter 1. Nevertheless, they have one.

Obviously, Tesla has a very different business model. What Tesla does is often the exact opposite of the established. And if it's not the opposite, Tesla tries to be as different as possible. This Nightmare Competitor simply built its own type of spacecraft and positioned it as an alternative to the established players' conventional spaceships.

No matter how different business models are, they rely on the same basic constituents. Anyone who's aware of these constituents can start to think systematically about how business models can be set apart; how totally different spaceships can be created. Compared to random ways of storytelling, this is a great advantage.

In, we convey the Business Model Constituents into our spaceship metaphor. The big spaceship stands for the established, while the small spacecraft represents the Nightmare Competitor. Both the spaceship and the spacecraft comprise the same Business Model Constituents. Let's get a feel for the constituents first before we analyze them in greater depth. The offering is what it is all about. It is what is provided to the customer. Without an offering, you don't have a business. In the space vessels, this is the payload that is placed at the very top.

Then, a value-creation system (internal, your own activities) and suppliers (external, delegated activities) are needed to create the offering. This is the central part of the rocket. Next, it is about utilization. It is the lever to drive down cost. The better this lever is used, the lower the price of the offering can be. This is why it is placed between the offering and the internal and external value-creation activities.

Making money is a central part of the business activities. Therefore, the model for generating revenues is placed throughout the center of the space vessels. Finally, it is about the Business Model Constituent standards of integrity. These standards are often underestimated, but they can differentiate business models so substantially that they become part of the offering. This is why they are represented as the hull of the vessels, like the offering.

There is one big difference between the spaceship of the established representing the industry and the much smaller spacecraft of the Nightmare Competitors: the spaceship of the established comprises additional boosters and external fuel tanks that are required to facilitate the much larger supporting systems.

BUSINESS MODEL CONSTITUENTS

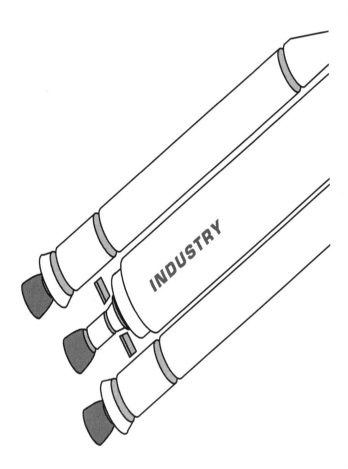

Diagram 1 *Spaceship of the Established and Spacecraft of a Nightmare Competitor with Business Model Constituents*

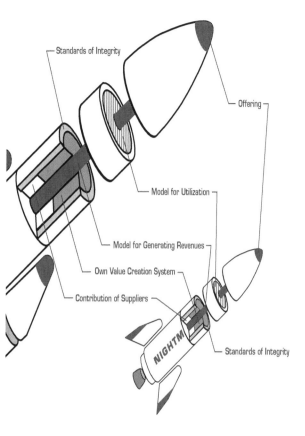

- Standards of Integrity
- Offering
- Model for Utilization
- Model for Generating Revenues
- Own Value Creation System
- Contribution of Suppliers
- Standards of Integrity

NIGHTM

Constituent 1 - Offerings

Any business model consists of an "offering" or a set of offerings. Offerings are products and services, features and functionality and their scope. The easiest way to identify what is offered by the established is to analyze how all the established players are promoting their offering. What do they claim on their websites and in their sales brochures? You can also single out offerings by simply listening to sales reps' pitches.

Earlier, when we introduced what the automotive industry is offering, we only referred to the range of models, features, and engine concepts. By thinking more carefully about offerings and by going through all their sales collateral, we might end up with other elements as well, like design and prestige, safety, fuel consumption, or purchasing options. This way, we enlarge the spectrum of offerings that can be questioned. As we've said, being systematic has its advantages.

You can practice describing offerings. Ask yourself what it is that all telecommunication companies are offering? What is it all banks are offering, all utilities, all premium watchmakers, all coffee companies, all companies offering a certain type of machinery, all consultants, all lawyers, all tax advisors, all facility-management companies? It's so obvious that it goes without saying.

While going through these examples, take a moment and think about the set of offerings in your own industry that are taken for granted. Could a Nightmare Competitor challenge what all players in your industry are offering as radically as Tesla is challenging the offerings of the automotive industry?

Constituent 2 - Value-Creation System

The "value-creation system" is the heart and soul of most companies. In the traditional sense of a business, this is where the machines are running and making noise, where it smells of oil, where workers sweat, or robots dance their mechanical ballet. But think about banks: everything required to handle money safely and interact with customers is part of their value-creation system. Scientifically, value-creation systems are defined as the sum of all internal activities that work to add value, such as production and logistics, the sales channels used, and all the activities to acquire and keep customers. Value-creation usually requires assets, processes, and competences.

If you struggle to define the value-creation system of the established, simply ask consultants from different consulting firms what it takes to be successful in the industry of interest. Consolidate what they say, and you'll have your starting point. In most cases, the discussion of the value-creation system does not require in-depth knowledge. Think about it. You can probably describe the value-creation system of your company with great ease.

In the systematic process of thinking, we are suggesting that you can now question the value-creation system and come up with alternatives. Tesla questioned the necessity of dealers, expensive marketing, and whether they should orchestrate as many suppliers as the established. They decided to establish their own charging infrastructure instead and could, initially at least, provide free access to it. This way, Tesla could ask potential customers whether they'd rather be subjected to advertisements or receive free battery charging.

One thing Tesla took care of at a very early stage was developing the capability to make updates and fixes remotely for the lifetime of each car via software. The direct relationship with customers and the extreme importance that software has in electric cars provides them with a perfect basis for this.

Let us propose more ideas even beyond the automotive industry as to how value-creation systems can be challenged. We hope this offers you support in questioning the value-creation system of your own industry.

Are branches really a prerequisite to offer banking services? Questioning this expensive infrastructure might have led to a value-creation system of online banks just as easily as the offering-related question of whether banking could be made more convenient. Do all fashion companies really need to dye garments in Asia to save the exorbitant cost for environmental protection in the Western world? Benetton began dying in close proximity to its most important markets. This enabled them to adjust their colors to meet market demands in no time. The change in the value-creation system was a prerequisite for the once-famous "United Colors of Benetton" story. A crucial question for defining the value-creation system of Cirque du Soleil regarded whether animals were necessary. This is an important consideration. After all, the animals are by far the most relevant cost position of any traditional circus.

In the context of value-creation systems, a great way to come up with new ideas is to ask what you could afford if you would eliminate or drastically reduce certain elements of the value-creation. The Spanish fashion company Zara doesn't participate in fashion shows, doesn't employ fancy designers, spends comparatively little on marketing, and is thereby able to finance a value-creation system allowing them to offer lots of collections a year.

What is the value-creation system each of the players within your industry has in place? Could anybody come up with a value-creation system as different as the companies we've discussed in this chapter?

Constituent 3 - Suppliers

"Suppliers" could be seen as an integral element of the value-creation process. However, we decided to see the suppliers as a separate category of constituents. One reason is that it allows us to see the internal world of value-creation and the external world, represented by the system of suppliers, separately. So, one side is about *making* and the other is about *buying*. The other reason for evaluating the suppliers separately is that some business systems today are rather defined by the supplier side or at least so heavily determined by the supplier side that they therefore deserve a separate evaluation.

Looking at our automotive case study, we can say that all the established players practice multiple sourcing. Tesla is cautious in employing suppliers. In crucial areas of the value-creation process, Tesla tries to limit its dependency on suppliers. But for many parts, such as power steering, brakes, and wheels, outsourcing remains a necessity nonetheless. This is another aspect we hadn't covered in our "Tesla-versus-the-automotive industry" narrative. It's not an extremely strong point, but thanks to the process of moving systematically from one Business Model Constituent to the next, the aspect of, "How do we deal with suppliers?" comes into play.

Let's delve into further examples of how the business model constituent suppliers is challenged in other industries. We hope these examples will provide you with ideas about how you can challenge the way suppliers are employed in your industry.

Consider the case of Airbnb, the Nightmare Competitor of the hotel industry. An important aspect of their business model is that Airbnb does not own a single bed. The same is true for Uber, the Nightmare Competitor of the taxi service industry. Uber does not own a single car. Spreadshirt, a German T-shirt company, allows users to create individualized T-shirts. The users can also sell their designs via Spreadshirt to the public. So, the company doesn't need to employ a single designer.

Making use of the crowd isn't the only way to create a totally different system of suppliers. Let's also pay tribute to one of the rare examples in which one of the established players did a great job in challenging the given. Germany's Lufthansa was one of the driving forces behind Star Alliance. The intercontinentally linked airlines of the alliance became mutual suppliers to each other. In a world that was rapidly becoming increasingly international, this was a crucial element of success.

Another example relevant to this discussion is Apple, which is well known for its awesome hardware, but unlike the established in its industry, it doesn't actually manufacture it. Apple broke ranks, deciding instead to employ a single supplier, Foxconn.

Zara is also a good example of a company that reversed an industry's typical distribution of work. The company is running its own production in its own factories, many located close to local markets, and is shipping directly to its own network of retail outlets. They started this practice when the advice of the consultants to the fashion industry was to outsource as much as possible.

These examples make it clear what can be achieved when the boundaries between your own value-creation process and a supplier's contribution are redefined. Could anybody in your industry come up with something as radically different as the examples we've listed?

Constituent 4 - Utilization

The fourth constituent dimension of business models is "utilization." The Tesla-versus-automobile-industry story has already shown how important the utilization of the value-creation system is. To utilize their own infrastructure and overheads, the established are trying to do whatever it takes to sell more cars. By selling more cars, they also provide a contribution to utilizing the value-creation system of suppliers and, therefore, get better deals. All are benefiting from the economies of scale created.

Tesla's approach to focus on the utilization of the production of the most expensive element of electro-mobility, the battery, is an extremely smart move. It provides the attacker with an advantage in the field that is most decisive for profitability when electro-mobility becomes a mass phenomenon.

Once again, we want to provide further ideas to make creative use of this Business Model Constituent. How can a Nightmare Competitor come up with a different business model by interpreting the constituent utilization differently?

SpaceX challenged the industry paradigm that rockets are single-use tools, launched to put satellites in orbit or connect us with the International Space Station. SpaceX has put great effort into creating reusable rockets. And they appear to be succeeding. The company can drive down the cost per launch far below what any of the competitors are able to offer. For SpaceX, the utilization of the product in use is as important, or maybe even more important than the utilization of the production. With this, SpaceX goes beyond the traditional playing field.

To go even further with the concept of making the most of assets, consider the idea of sharing goods and services. Machinery sharing is a very old system. Farmers, for instance, have been sharing expensive and seldom-used equipment for ages. They founded cooperatives to take care of purchasing the assets and utilizing them.

It took some time before companies understood the potential of sharing. NetJets saw potential in making small planes available for more users and founded an executive jet-sharing service that has grown to a 700-strong fleet. Similarly, car-sharing services provide access to a vehicle without the hassles and expenses of ownership.

Be creative in what you can utilize. Amazon is a grand master of utilization, having famously utilized its infrastructure for selling books. The Internet giant is hardly even perceived as a book vendor anymore. Brands can open up their webshops on the Amazon platform. The company charges them a tidy sum for the exposure to its own traffic, but they don't stop there. Amazon Web Services offers cloud services as a way of utilizing its gigantic server infrastructure in the best way possible. Ask yourself what the model for utilization is used by all the players in your industry. How would a potential Nightmare Competitor to your industry make use of this Business Model Constituent?

Constituent 5 - Model for Generating Revenues

The fifth constituent of business models, the "model for generating revenues," needs no justification. Each business needs at least enough revenues to finance its activities and necessary investments. There isn't a business around that isn't striving for even more. After all, shareholders have expectations, too.

As with all the constituents, we're discussing whether this Business Model Constituent can contribute to complete the Tesla-versus-the-automotive-industry case. All the players in the automotive industry are offering leasing and financing solutions. For them, it has become a very important element of their business model. It doesn't take much to come up with financing solutions, and Tesla is offering them, as well. Regarding the Business Model Constituent model for generating revenues, Tesla is not reinventing the world.

If you want to develop ideas to challenge the Model for Generating Revenues in your industry, also ask yourself whether a Nightmare Competitor can charge for something different than each of the established players in the industry?

Traditional airlines try to charge as much as possible for each ticket, whereas Michael O'Leary, CEO of Ryanair, has repeatedly spoken about his aspiration of making flying free of charge. What sounds like a PR stunt is, at its core, very interesting. Ryanair is receiving incentives from municipalities and regions with smaller airports, eager to get more tourists. The company is also making money on the basis of associated services. They receive commissions for airport transfers, car rentals, sightseeing tours, and so on. Additionally, they've been making money by buying their identical planes in large quantities and, therefore, getting enormous rebates. Depending on the market situation, the planes can be sold for a profit after a relatively short period of use.

The newspaper business can also serve as an example. Newspapers have always followed a model in which advertising generates revenues. These revenues allow them to sell newspapers at lower prices to their readers. The so-called, "free" newspapers went a step further. Advertisers are footing the bill completely. The value-creation system is designed to allow that because companies are able to reach potential customers at metro stations before they start their commute. A specific target audience is reached with specific content and product ads in a situation where they have nothing else to do. Because the audience of interest can be addressed so perfectly, companies that want to market their offerings to this audience are ready to pay a premium.

Advertising revenues are a powerful source. If you use Google's search engine, you don't pay when you type in search criteria, nor are you charged a subscription fee. You don't pay at all, in fact, at least not in a traditional sense of payment, meaning money. However, by providing your data to the company, you are giving Google something that it values as much, if not more, than money.

Another way of coming up with a substantially different model to generate revenues is by changing the structure of pricing. For example, lawyers are traditionally paid by the hour. Even a ten-year-old child is able to understand there is therefore no incentive to work efficiently. If offered to be paid by the hour, the child will take their time to get the job done. As you might expect therefore, nobody in the legal world is actively engaged in changing this paradigm. What about marketers, coaches, and consultants? The predominant model for generating money prevents the established players from thinking creatively about the given business model. A newcomer, if allowed access, is not bound by that. Professions with regulatory entry barriers should be cautious. From a strategic perspective, it can never be really satisfying to be dependent on barriers for others to enter. If newcomers can show they can provide a better performance, Pandora's Box is opened.

The most radical way of thinking about the model for generating revenues leads back to the Business Model Constituent offering. Should doctors charge for trying to cure patients or for keeping them healthy? Should music companies charge for CDs or for music? Should companies producing heaters or air conditioners charge for their hardware or for providing a desired temperature?

Think about it. Could outsiders bring your industry out of balance by introducing substantially different models for generating revenues?

Constituent 6 - Standards of Integrity

Finally, customers need to be able to understand companies. Consistency in word and deed is required. This leads us to "standards of integrity," the sixth and last constituent of business models.

Wikipedia defines integrity as, "The inner sense of wholeness deriving from qualities such as honesty and consistency of character." Furthermore, the encyclopedia states, "As such, one may judge that others 'have integrity' to the extent that they act according to the values, beliefs, and principles they claim to hold."

In the context of our automotive example, the constituent integrity compels us to ask how much integrity can an automotive company possess when it's selling electric cars with the intention to make green customers happy, but simultaneously providing gas-guzzling monsters and investing heavily in motor sports? There's a good chance that conscious consumers will perceive this as disingenuous.

As you can already see, this last constituent of business

models reaches into areas that tend to make established companies uncomfortable. But therein lies enormous potential for Nightmare Competitors. The following examples should encourage you to be as radical as possible as you attempt to develop an understanding of the impact a Nightmare Competitor could have by making use of this potential.

Compare traditional cosmetic companies with The Body Shop, which declared in 1976 that it wouldn't sell or use products or ingredients that were tested on animals. This was long before any of the established even considered animal rights. And they have kept that promise.

Established banks have figured out how to earn a lot of money by inventing new financial products and churning the portfolios of their customers. They promise that the new financial products will provide a much higher dividend or rate of interest than that which they sold a few months earlier. In reality, the reason for this is that every sale leads to a commission, whether it benefits the customer or not. Objective advice is not incentivized by this model, and bankers with high-variable compensation might struggle to define what to put first: their bonus or their customers' well-being. By contrast, one modern German bank, Quirinbank, refrains from the commission-based model. Quirinbank charges for the advice, but pays all commissions back to customers.

The food industry is an obvious target as an example in the context of integrity. How much integrity can a food company have when it sells both genetically modified foods and organic foods? How much integrity can a food company have when it sells sugar-crusted caloric bombs, as well as nutrient-dense, healthy products? And the low point in terms of integrity is reached when products that need to be seen as unhealthy are sold as a valuable contribution to the diet of children. Different branding might help on the surface. However, no matter what they do to disguise their true conduct, these companies are enormously vulnerable. Customers are not stupid, and with the advent of the Internet, they have better access to information on which to base their judgments.

Given the definition of integrity we provided, Ryanair is a totally integral company. People might complain about the low level of service they're offering in contrast with other airlines. Some might even talk about inconveniences they expect their customers to endure. If Ryanair's intention is to make flying as cheap as possible, then "no frills" should be taken seriously. That's what they do, and they don't leave anybody in the dark about it. They're consistent in word and deed. So, keep in mind that integrity doesn't need to be equated with high moral ground. The hurdle for integrity is actually lower.

What's the reason for this lack of integrity on the side of the incumbents? As previously discussed, established businesses need to grow because they're fighting for economies of scale. Therefore, they open their doors to almost any type of customer. This makes it difficult to be consistent. The more difficult or even impossible it is to name the standards of integrity of established companies, the better the opportunities for attackers to shine brightly.

Ask yourself how outsiders could bring your industry out of balance by introducing substantially different standards of integrity?

We want to convince you that it makes sense to go through each of the Business Model Constituents one by one. The enhancements we could make to the story of Tesla-versus-the-automotive-industry are quite substantial. The already-convincing story we started with became more comprehensive and complete. For the process of developing alternative business models systematically, this is of great significance. However, there is still room for improvement.

Ultimately, we want a tool that allows us to grasp and display the beauty of an alternative business model at a glance. This is relevant for the process of developing business models, but is also of greatest importance when it comes to communicating the potential of a competing business model. Others need to be able to understand and memorize what's been presented. Therefore, it's necessary to be able to extract the essence of business models and visualize them. The Business Model Radar we're going to introduce in the next section allows us to meet these objectives.

THE BUSINESS MODEL RADAR

The importance radar has had in military history can hardly be overemphasized. During the battles of World War II, airplanes became decisive. With their increased range and payload capabilities, they could carry massively destructive bombs further across enemy lines and into a nation's cities. Therefore, it became crucial to detect the movements of the rival air forces.

Scientists worked feverishly on the evolution of this passive weapon and even advanced it beyond the skies. No longer constrained to pure airborne applications, radar made it possible to win battles by being the first to spot ships or submarines, not just airplanes, consider their plans, and respond by deploying assaults or countermeasures that would previously have been impossible.

Inspired by the contribution that radar had and still has in terms of winning battles in the military domain, we developed a tool that provides the same contribution for business model innovation. Paying tribute to great invention and to provide you with an *aide-memoire*, it should not come as a surprise that we named our tool the "Business Model Radar" or that it actually resembles a radar screen.

Diagram 2 shows the basic structure of our Business Model Radar.

On the basis of a blank Business Model Radar, it's now possible to come up with graphical representations of the position the established take over in their industry. All you

DIAGRAM 2
BUSINESS MODEL RADAR
Basic Structure

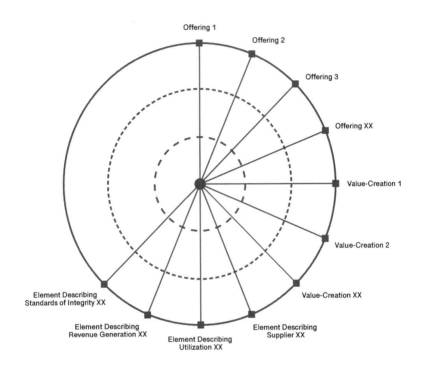

Offering 1
Offering 2
Offering 3
Offering XX
Value-Creation 1
Value-Creation 2
Value-Creation XX
Element Describing Supplier XX
Element Describing Utilization XX
Element Describing Revenue Generation XX
Element Describing Standards of Integrity XX

Low Importance − − − −	Offering (O)
Medium Importance − − − − − −	Value-Creation System (V)
High Importance ▬▬▬▬	Suppliers (S)
	Model for Utilisation (U)
	Model for Generating Revenues (R)
	Standards of Integrity (I)

need to do is to place the elements you have identified as being of great importance to their business model while systematically following through the Business Model Constituents at the outer rim of the Business Model Radar.

We refer to such a graphical representation as a profile. Let's see what a profile of an established looks like. By now, you're familiar with all the details of the story of Tesla's assault on the automotive industry. Therefore, it makes sense to stick with this story and start by profiling the auto industry.

The automotive industry is characterized by the *offerings*: Range of Models, Features & Engine Concepts, Design and Prestige, and Purchasing Options. Under *value-creation system*, elements like the Dealers, the Extensive Marketing, or the function as an Orchestrator of suppliers can be positioned. Since multiple *suppliers* are used, we can also note Multiple Sources. The constituent *utilization* leads us to Economies of Scale on the basis of Cars Sold. *Revenues* are made via Selling Cars & Financing and After-Sales Service. As already discussed, there are no specific elements under the constituent *integrity*.

Since it's about pointing out what the incumbents are proud of, all the elements describing the established are positioned at the outer rim.

In the same way, using the Business Model Constituents, the profile of already-existing Nightmare Competitors can be plotted. However, the greatest achievement of the

DIAGRAM 3
BUSINESS MODEL RADAR
Automotive Industry Profile

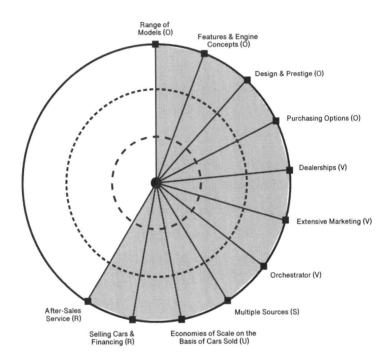

Range of Models (O)
Features & Engine Concepts (O)
Design & Prestige (O)
Purchasing Options (O)
Dealerships (V)
Extensive Marketing (V)
Orchestrator (V)
Multiple Sources (S)
Economies of Scale on the Basis of Cars Sold (U)
Selling Cars & Financing (R)
After-Sales Service (R)

■ Automotive Industry

Low Importance	– – –	Offering (O)
Medium Importance	– – – – –	Value-Creation System (V)
High Importance	——————	Suppliers (S)
		Model for Utilisation (U)
		Model for Generating Revenues (R)
		Standards of Integrity (I)

Business Model Radar is that it allows you to identify how potential Nightmare Competitors can position themselves. The Business Model Radar makes it possible to go to the extreme and to think in opposites. The full force of potential attacks becomes apparent.

Let's try to draw a profile displaying the essence of the now-familiar Tesla story.

The Nightmare Competitor's Range of Models is quite limited. The same is true for the Features & Engine Concepts. Design/Prestige are relevant for Tesla just like they are for the established. Purchasing Options are offered but not to the same extent. The offerings of the established, which are not important to Tesla, become directly visible in the diagram.

Regarding the value-creation system, it's safe to say that Tesla doesn't rely on Dealers, spends relatively little money on Marketing, and that they're less of an Orchestrator than the established. Consequently, they rely on less suppliers. Tesla can't compete in the Economies of Scale game in terms of cars sold. However, just like the established, they earn money via Selling Cars & Financing. In direct contrast with the established, they don't rely on earning money via After Sales Service.

As opposed to the established, Tesla's offer is Cars for Environmental Leadership and a Charging Infrastructure. With their own Stores and Galleries and the ability to take care of Remote Updates and Fixes, they have their

DIAGRAM 4
BUSINESS MODEL RADAR
Tesla vs. Automotive Industry

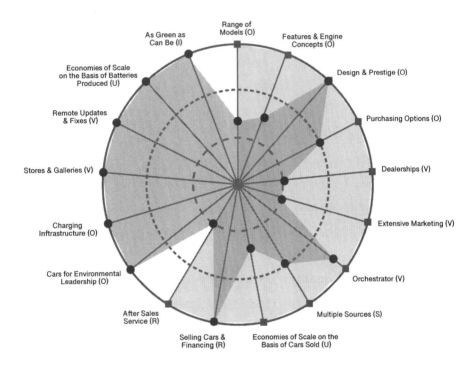

- ● Tesla
- ■ Automotive Industry

Low Importance	– – –	Offering (O)
Medium Importance	– – – – –	Value-Creation System (V)
High Importance	——	Suppliers (S)
		Model for Utilisation (U)
		Model for Generating Revenues (R)
		Standards of Integrity (I)

Labels around the radar:

- As Green as Can Be (I)
- Range of Models (O)
- Features & Engine Concepts (O)
- Economies of Scale on the Basis of Batteries Produced (U)
- Design & Prestige (O)
- Remote Updates & Fixes (V)
- Purchasing Options (O)
- Stores & Galleries (V)
- Dealerships (V)
- Charging Inftrastructure (O)
- Extensive Marketing (V)
- Cars for Environmental Leadership (O)
- Orchestrator (V)
- After Sales Service (R)
- Multiple Sources (S)
- Selling Cars & Financing (R)
- Economies of Scale on the Basis of Cars Sold (U)

specific elements of a value-creation system. They achieve Economies of Scale by the utilization of their battery factory. And finally, they take care of integrity, since they are as Green as Can Be.

This diagram, which paints a picture of the differences between the profile of the established and of the attacker, saves a thousand words. Newcomers have no problem eliminating what is considered holy by the established. Due to the elimination, enormous cost savings and efficiency gains become possible. They allow the intruders to over perform in new dimensions. It should be apparent that the established are in jeopardy.

SLEEPLESS NIGHTS

Readers experienced in business modeling can probably identify the authors who inspired us in creating the Business Model Radar. Chan Kim and Renée Mauborgne enlightened us with their landmark book, *Blue Ocean Strategy* in 2005. And we pay tribute to Alexander Osterwalder and Yves Pigneur and the ideas they introduced with their book, *Business Model Generation* in 2010. We experimented with both approaches for quite some time but were never completely satisfied with the results. That gave us sleepless nights.

The Blue Ocean approach doesn't provide a structure for identifying elements of business models systematically. While Osterwalder's and Pigneur's Business Model Canvas does provide such a structure, we missed the chance to map opposing business models. We started to merge the methods and, in the process, became aware that further amendments were required.

The Business Model Canvas contains customer segments. However, we think it's important to keep customer segments separate. The segments are not part of the business model; the business models need to be designed to serve certain customer segments and, as such, the customer segments need to be defined before the business model is described. For us, utilization and integrity are too important not to be taken into account on the utmost level. Therefore, we developed something we find better serves the purpose, which you are now familiar with: the Business Model Constituents.

There's another thing that kept us awake. Even though Clayton Christensen, in his book, *The Innovator's Dilemma: When New Technologies Cause Great Firms to Fail* kicked off the whole business innovation movement back in 1997, very little of what he describes as the innovator's dilemma has found its way into all the other books that followed in the aftermath.

No matter whether we take *Blue Ocean, Business Model Generation*, Mark Johnson's *Seizing the White Space* or other books of authors of the same league, all of them praise the beauty of creating new business models. But this does not seem to help the established introduce such business models and thereby define the future of their industries.

And why? Because they are caught in their own business models just as we described with the corporate spaceship analogy in the first chapter.

We asked ourselves repeatedly, "How is it possible to rock the corporate spaceships?" One of our breakthrough moments occurred after intense dialogues with psychologists, who brought us to an unexpected realization. They made us aware that fear is a much greater motivator than opportunity. It was programmed in our brain in the times when our ancestors lived in caves. As soon as we sense danger, adrenaline is injected into our blood and our whole body becomes alert. Our predecessors were feverishly searching for strategies that would lead them out of the calamity. The classic "fight or flight" response is a result of this. These patterns of response remain in us still. It's impossible to create the same level of alertness with the sweetest of opportunities.

It dawned on us that we needed to confront the managers of established organizations with the consequences of what will happen if they don't manage to think beyond their own business models. This is how the corporate spaceship analogy and the Nightmare Competitor approach were born. By now, we take it as a compliment when managers call to tell us that we've deprived them of their sleep and that these nightmares keep coming back to them night after night. It means we've managed to create a level of awareness that was not there before.

The nightmares the managers are struggling with might have recurring elements but vary nevertheless. The explanation for this is that industries are commonly attacked by more than one single Nightmare Competitor. Therefore, the dreams are messy and the minds of the managers are working overtime to make something intelligible out of it.

Properly understanding the various types of attacks would provide an enormous step forward. It would be possible to bring structure into the messiness. The danger arising out of each attack could be assessed. It would be possible to develop strategies to fight the attackers or to occupy the space before they had the chance to become creepy.

Such a state of awareness and preparedness we define as "Intellectual Leadership." This Intellectual Leadership is the basis for returning to regular sleep patterns. In the following chapter, we'll show you how you can obtain Intellectual Leadership.

③

INTELLECTUAL
LEADERSHIP

We've discussed the threat Tesla provides for the traditional automotive industry in quite some detail. But as already suggested, Tesla is not the established carmakers *only* Nightmare Competitor.

Chinese cars with internal combustion engines never matched the cars of their Western, Japanese, or Korean rivals. It might well be that Chinese manufacturers will catch up and even overtake their rivals in the new game. The Chinese government is radically pushing electro-mobility. They took great care that local producers are well prepared for the dawning age of electro-mobility, and the introduction and enforcement of their own China-specific standards will help them to succeed. Taking this level of determination and their foresight into account, and given the basis their gigantic market provides for generating economies of scale, they have all it takes to become the leaders in the field of electro-mobility internationally. Maybe this aim is as important to the Chinese Government as solving their pollution and energy-dependency issues.

With Carplay, Apple has found its way into the automotive world. The digital offerings of Apple and its rivals are likely to substitute speed and acceleration as purchasing criteria. With their products and services, they are in direct contact with end users in a time when traditional players are still struggling to get the email addresses of their customers right. Some of these players are also in a very strong position when it comes to enabling vehicles to drive autonomously. There is a danger that traditional car companies end up being hardware manufacturers for the newbies.

Singapore and Dubai are testing electrically propelled drones that can carry passengers. Startups like U.S.-based Hoversurf and China-based Ehang have furthered the development of such drones to a point in which commercial use becomes feasible. For the privileged, such drones might be fancier toys than Ferraris and Porsches.

Congested and suffocating cities are also a problem in other regions of the world. City planners are experimenting intensely with concepts making it possible to reduce the number of cars in cities. Cable cars for public city transport are one of the alternatives. Customers have privacy in their cabins. With gondolas arriving in short sequence, waiting times could be eradicated. In the future, cable-car producers like Doppelmayr and Leitner might produce the alternatives to small city cars.

For some time, car-sharing seemed to be a big trend. Even some incumbents jumped onto it. Car2go, for example, is offering Mercedes and Smart cars, DriveNow is offering BMWs and Minis. But who needs *extra* cars for carpooling services when existing cars can be used to share rides? BlaBlaCar, Ridesharing, and Coseats have established such services for long distances. Whereas companies like Uber and Lyft make use of existing cars and their drivers to focus more on shorter rides.

A company called Double Robotics is approaching the market from a totally different angle: they are offering awesome telepresence robots for telecommuters. The "Double," as the robot is called, seems to consist of an iPad mounted on a Segway with a broomstick. The robots can be driven remotely through offices and the drivers are even able to engage in hallway conversations. Double Robotics' intention is to create a "better than being there" teleconferencing experience. For managers who see traveling as a time-consuming evil, the Double becomes an alternative to business trips, many of which would otherwise be taken in cars. And digital natives will love it, too, regardless of profession.

It is amazing how many different types of players can be seen as Nightmare Competitors to the automotive industry. But despite it all, the industry has done little to attain Intellectual Leadership. Do the managers of the automotive industry even sleep poorly? They are starting to. Some of them belong to the ones that call us to talk about their unsettling sleep patterns.

What is the reason it took them so long? Maybe the ongoing success of their current business model has worked like a strong sleeping pill. Another explanation is that their competitive intelligence systems were attuned to their industry peers and not to players that don't even have the ambition to be seen as part of the automotive industry. However, the strongest reason is probably that they don't take the small players seriously enough. The number of small players and their heterogeneity makes it difficult to deal with them. But every little bit counts: be aware that a loss of 10 percent in sales in most industries makes the difference between heaven and hell. For an industry as crazily determined by economies of scale as the automotive industry, this is especially true.

No matter what industry we're talking about, the only way to avoid getting caught with your pants down is to attain Intellectual Leadership. But how? What we've discussed so far may have already provided an idea. It's not about what *we* as established companies do and strive for. It's about what *others* might be doing to become more attractive to our customers. And the easiest way to win the hearts of customers is to be more attuned to what they truly want.

CUSTOMER-CENTRIC BUSINESS MODELING

We've identified five groups of customers whom the established regularly underserve, making them highly attractive to Nightmare Competitors.

Group number one consists of customers who have become bored with the offerings of the established. In the beginning, they liked the features and functionalities the established launched in regular intervals. But the permanent improvement of something they now take for granted doesn't provide them with kicks anymore. They're looking for something special. Therefore, we've given them the name, "Unique Value Customers." Unique Value Customers are not especially price sensitive. Either they are affluent or they are willing to save up to buy something that provides them with a kick. Unique Value Customers are attractive for another reason: they're often opinion leaders in their field. Others imitate what they do. Few trends are set without the involvement of these outstanding personalities.

The established always enjoy serving the upper end of the market. But these customers don't necessarily want to be seen as the upper end of something; they want to be seen as special. This is where the economies-of-scale-based business model of the established reaches its limits.

At the other end of the spectrum is the "Bargain Customer." These customers are tighter than a duck's bum. If the price can be reduced, they're ready to get their hands dirty to make it happen. They're okay with waiting in line, and they accept bland design, as well as base-model products and services lacking features and functionalities, bells, and whistles. However, the quality of the core offering still needs to be good. They're not ready to accept crap.

They don't mind being considered bargain hunters. They regard themselves as being smarter than their peers who fall for the superficial promises of the premium brands. They read review magazines to make sure they're getting a good deal. Bargain Customers are quite immune to advertising. They're aware they're the ones footing the bill for that flashy ad campaign, after all. The only advertising they're interested in involve ads in which the everyday price is slashed and substituted with a remarkably lower one.

Traditional companies don't tend to focus exclusively on Bargain Customers. It's only when the established need to dump stock that these customers are welcomed for the contribution margin they can provide. Otherwise, the established prefer to service more upmarket customers.

Yet another kind of customer is the "Choice Customer." This person is interested in transparency. They want to see what types of products are available on the market, ideally on a worldwide basis. They want to see how much stock is on hand or be informed about the availability of services. Of course, they're interested in price transparency, as well. Here, Choice Customers and Bargain Customers mingle. Choice customers see the Internet as mankind's greatest invention. It allows them to follow their passion. And the ubiquity of the Internet has led them to the conviction that total transparency of all offerings and their respective prices are a fundamental right.

The Choice Customer is completely outside the scope of the established, who try to make their lives as difficult as possible or at least attempt to seduce them so they don't follow their basic instincts.

The fourth type of customer is the "Ultimate Want Customer." Ultimate Want Customers were never really happy with what the industry had to offer. Who wants insurance or who wants to see a doctor? However, the larger percentage of the Ultimate Want Customers are not aware of the offerings being workarounds and fixes. But as soon as any Ultimate Want Customer gets closer to being offered a carefree life without insurance or health without doctors, then they understand that what they never previously questioned was actually not the best solution for them. Offered an alternative, these Ultimate Want Customers are gone in the blink of an eye. They ask themselves why it took so long for anybody to come up with such an alternative.

This type of customer is not outside the scope of the established. But when the customer discovers an alternative and becomes disloyal, it's enormously difficult to win them back. Often, a totally different business model is required

The final type is the "Access Customer," who is not yet

even a customer. The industry isn't aware of the possibility of a relationship or considers it beneath its dignity to serve such customers. No matter whether it's negligence or intent, it goes without saying that this type of customer is outside of the scope of the traditional players. The only problem for the established is that anybody building a business model to attract Access Customers might also attract some of their customers.

The great advantage Nightmare Competitors have is that they're fancy-free. Their DNA isn't necessarily determined by a technological invention. They don't need or want to make everybody happy. The Nightmare Competitor can focus completely on making specific types of customers happy, and to that end, they can create specific business models.

Taking the five distinct customer groups into account makes creating Nightmare Competitors even easier than described in Chapter 2. Customer-Centric Business Models are created in four steps.

The process starts with something that is almost a no-brainer after everything we've discussed already. However, **Step 1** is important for being systematic. It's about describing the customer base of the established. Since the established are usually serving a broad spectrum of customers, it is usually just a matter of writing down "everybody," "all customers," or something along that line. So, Step 1 can often be carried out within seconds.

Step 2 is something you're already familiar with. Step 2 describes the business model the industry has honed over time to serve their broad target group as perfectly as possible. And the result of the description should be a profile of the business model of the established. You've already learned how to profile the incumbents. Take the Business Model Constituents offering, value-creation system, suppliers, model for utilization, model for generating revenues, and standards of integrity, and for each of these constituents,

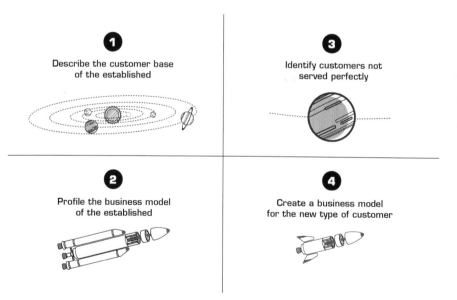

①
Describe the customer base
of the established

③
Identify customers not
served perfectly

②
Profile the business model
of the established

④
Create a business model
for the new type of customer

The Four Steps for Creating Customer-Centric Business Models

think about the best elements characterizing the business model of the industry. Diagram 3 illustrates this process. Position the findings in the Business Model Radar just as we've done with the automotive industry in v.

Step 3 is the most important step in Customer-Centric Business Modeling. It's about identifying the customer groups not being served perfectly. Here, the five types of customers we've identified above are relevant. They are of special interest for Nightmare Competitors. Having these predefined customer groups should help you get started. That they are predefined doesn't mean they are limiting the creative process. For example, there are several ways to provide unique value. Abercrombie & Fitch identified customers who saw a special shopping experience as a unique value. Zara focuses on a totally different unique value, giving customers the chance to find new items every time they go shopping. So, the five types of customers merely provide orientation and structure. Think of it as having flexibility within a framework. Whenever you feel it might be helpful to go beyond the predefined groups of customers to assess or create a Nightmare Competitor, give it a try. However, we've made the experience that this is hardly ever necessary.

In **Step 4**, we create business models for the new types of customers. Obviously, each of the customer groups needs to be addressed with a specific business model. The objective of Step 4 is to end up with profiles describing these specific business models. Each of these business models and the corresponding profiles describe a Nightmare Competitor.

We're following the same process to create these business models. First, we define the core offering for the specified type of customer. Then, we challenge the given business model of the established. Taking the type of customer and the core offering into account, we ask what's really necessary? In the process of challenging what's been taken for granted, we almost automatically end up with new ideas for what the Nightmare Competitor could do differently. However, to systematically identify new elements, it makes sense to use the Business Model Constituents once again. Ask yourself, with regard to each constituent, what elements could be added to set the new business model apart from the business of the established? Position the findings in the Business Model Radar, connect the dots, and you've got a profile of a Nightmare Competitor.

The Business Model Radar displaying the profile of the established in relation to the profile of the Nightmare Competitor shows then how the latter can use laser-sharp customer focus to turn the assets of the former into liabilities and perceived strengths into weaknesses.

Now, if this sounds a bit too theoretical, don't worry. In the following sections, we'll introduce plenty of examples of Nightmare Competitors that are serving the customer types defined above perfectly. These examples will make you more familiar with the process of Customer-Centric Business Modeling.

ASSESSING ARCHETYPES OF ATTACKERS

To make life easier, we've named the Nightmare Competitors after the five types of customers.

Unique Value Nightmare Competitors provide bored customers with new kicks. Bargain Nightmare Competitors offer the radical budget offerings that draw price-sensitive customers. Choice Nightmare Competitors provide transparency and make a vast number of offerings available. Ultimate Want Nightmare Competitors provide attractive alternatives that make the offerings of the established look like work-arounds. Access Nightmare Competitors provide a chance to participate for all those who were formerly implicitly or explicitly excluded by the industry. Access Nightmare Competitors cause damage even though they do not address the customers of the established directly. However, as soon as customers of the established start to find their offering appealing, they need to be seen as Nightmare Competitors, too.

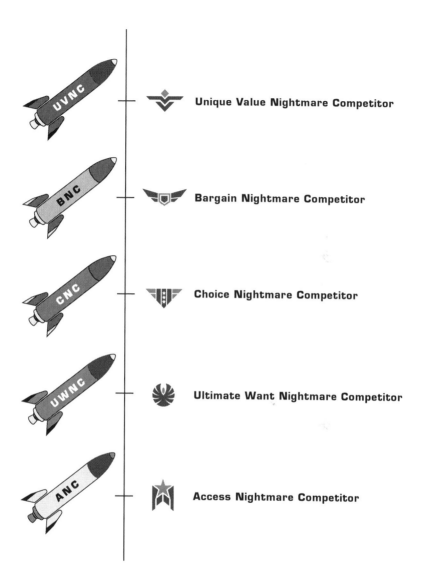

The Five Attacker Archetypes

Unique Value Nightmare Competitor

Bargain Nightmare Competitor

Choice Nightmare Competitor

Ultimate Want Nightmare Competitor

Access Nightmare Competitor

The Unique Value Nightmare Competitor

Perhaps without even realizing it, you've already learned a great deal about Unique Value Nightmare Competitors. Tesla is one.

Isn't Tesla serving the Unique Value Customers perfectly? Tesla helps these customers express themselves while providing something they cherish and can't stop talking about. Tesla is taking care of customers who are bored with the offerings of the established. These customers aren't price sensitive and are often opinion leaders in their field.

The explanation of Tesla as the Nightmare Competitor of the automotive industry becomes even easier with the customer perspective in mind.

Following the process of Customer-Centric Business Modeling systematically, we start with defining "everybody" as the customer served by the car manufacturers. This is as easy as announced earlier on and can indeed be done in seconds. In Step 2, we describe the establisheds' business model for making everybody happy. It is the one we have already discussed and profiled in Diagram 4.

In Step 3, we define the Unique Value Customers. There are lots of people out there who are not fans of Tesla. They see Elon Musk as a braggart. In their eyes, Tesla's environmental aspiration is nothing but an empty promise. They might forecast Tesla's fall from grace. They might assume that the company will soon be notorious for the ruins of a gigantic factory they abandoned in Nevada as a testimony of their megalomania. But Tesla owners and "would-be" owners are of a distinctively different opinion. And that alone is what is relevant to Tesla.

Why should Tesla care about all the skeptics if there are enough people out there sharing their point of view? So, try to refrain from making your own personal values and beliefs the yardstick for evaluating the potential of business models. The only relevant question when it comes to assessing Nightmare Competitors is whether they can sustain their business model by providing a home for a sufficient number of people.

So, how can we name Tesla's Unique Value Customers? What about "The Affluent Green" or "Tree Huggers," if you prefer? Having defined customers in such a pointed way, it is usually very easy to challenge the status quo and come up with new elements. However, since we have spent quite some effort in analyzing Tesla's business model already, we can come back to that. The completed story with the profiles as well as the customer descriptions is now displayed in Diagram 6. The names of the two types of customers are stated in the boxes on the lower left side of the illustration. In all cases studies that we discuss in the following, we will stay true to this format.

Having enemies is almost a precondition for being a good

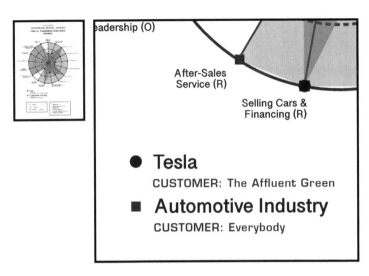

adership (O)

After-Sales
Service (R)

Selling Cars &
Financing (R)

● **Tesla**
   CUSTOMER: The Affluent Green

■ **Automotive Industry**
   CUSTOMER: Everybody

Diagram 6 *Business Model Radar with Profile of Tesla versus Profile of the Automotive Industry and Respective Customer Groups*

Unique Value Nightmare Competitor. Being vanilla does not create fans, believers, followers, or evangelists. Having an opinion about something does. Fighting for a cause does. Having your own ways does. So, the Unique Value Nightmare Competitor is the direct opposite of the "make everybody happy" approach we've discussed so critically.

What other companies can be named as examples for Unique Value Nightmare Competitors?

Apple was definitely a Unique Value Nightmare Competitor. We don't need to bore you with descriptions of the great deeds and general awesomeness of the company. By now, they're more of an established player, anyway. However, in the context of what we've described, we need to pay tribute to their laser-sharp focus on Unique Value Customers. Apple has never really served the lower end of the market. It hasn't succumbed to the temptation of making compromises for serving the corporate world. And this has brought them to where they are today. However, we'd like to see Tim Cook wake up and stop living off the shirt tails of Steve Jobs. He should instead be thinking about how he could be rocking the corporate ship he turned Apple into.

Hoversurf or Ehang, the two manufacturers of electrical drones for transporting people, are more recent and, therefore, probably better examples than Apple.

The examples of Tesla, Apple, and the drone companies could suggest that Unique Value Nightmare Competitors are companies solely operating at the upper end of the market. Although generally true, this isn't always the case. Zara, the Spanish fashion company, has provided unique, unprecedented value to its customers by offering them new fashionable items on an almost weekly basis. Compared to the high-end brands, Zara is inexpensive. But Zara is no Bargain Nightmare Competitor. This field is occupied by companies like H&M.

What about Starbucks? By now, we assume you should be able to tell the Starbucks story on your own. Give it a shot: get out a pen and paper and start to define the customer of the established, describe their business model, then define Starbucks' target customer and their business model.

Unique Value Nightmare Competitors are still offering products: cars, phones, computers, fashion items, or coffee. And it is about customers exchanging the product they've been using for the product of the Unique Value Nightmare Competitor. Because of this, the Unique Value Nightmare Competitor isn't the most exotic of the Attacker Archetypes. Nevertheless, Unique Value Nightmare Competitors are capable of carving out relevant slices of each incumbent's pie.

The only way to fight a Unique Value Nightmare Competitor that has already positioned itself is to provide the unique value customers with something that becomes their new object of affection. The smarter option might be to occupy the space before a potential Nightmare Competitor can.

The Bargain Nightmare Competitor

There's an inherent trait that unites all staff members of Bargain Nightmare Competitors from the top to the bottom of the hierarchy. All employees of Bargain Nightmare Competitors have an aversion to paying more than is absolutely necessary. It's their passion to find the best bargain; it's built into their DNA. They can't help themselves; they can't do anything about having this disposition.

IKEA founder, Ingvar Kamprad, with a reported personal net worth in excess of $3 billion USD, is famous for visiting his local markets shortly before closing time to scoop up bargains. This was at a time when the vendors for vegetables, fruits, and other perishable goods sold two for the price of one. To get to business meetings, IKEA employees have to meet at airports to create groups of four to drive in small rental cars to their destinations. Theo Albrecht, one of the founders of Aldi, was famous for driving around in a battered old Mercedes. If your ambition as a high school graduate is to fly business class around the world, there's only one piece of advice we can give you: apply for a job elsewhere.

And what they see as important for themselves, the employees of Bargain Nightmare Competitors provide for their customers. They build business models focused on one thing: the lowest possible price.

In the beginning, Aldi had just one thousand products. All of them were unbranded or, in other words, white label or generic products. Customers had to take them directly from the transport pallets. The cashiers had to know the codes of all the products by heart. Credit cards weren't accepted. The outlets had a dull standard design. The employee work ethic and discipline were unparalleled.

What can we learn from well-known Bargain Nightmare Competitors like Ikea and Aldi?

Usually, the product range is limited. The processes are simplified. Customized options are not given. Customers have to help themselves. Service is reduced to a minimum. Amazing, isn't it? The story of the Bargain Nightmare Competitors is a story best told by what they *don't* do. Would any customer survey have led to such a result? Hard to imagine that customers would beg not to have all the things the established spoil them with.

By now, we find Bargain Nightmare Competitors in many industries: budget banks, budget insurance companies, budget mobile phone providers, budget cars, budget clothes, and so on. There are also Bargain Nightmare Competitors in the business to business (B2B) segment. One is SpaceX, the U.S. aerospace manufacturer and space transport services company. Traditionally, for NASA to launch anything into space, just once, could cost anywhere from $100 million to $260 million USD. In contrast, at the time of writing this book, a SpaceX rocket launch costs around $60 million USD. The bargain offering is made possible by a complete focus on price-sensitive customers, the exclusion of traditional high-end suppliers, extreme modularity, and the reusability of parts of the rockets.

Other examples include Mindray, in the field of medical technology, and Honeywell, in the area of gas detection, as both have achieved low-price positions by providing products that are "good enough," as opposed to having all the bells and whistles certain customers don't need. But it's not about B2B or business to consumer (B2C). The fundamental question is whether the established are overshooting in terms of what customers actually need.

Think about your digital camera, your laptop computer, the programs you use on your computer, any modern TV set, or the options available on GPS systems. For many customers, the bells and whistles are more of a curse than a blessing. And with every feature and option, the established are adding another layer of expensive complexity. Happy days for Bargain Nightmare Competitors.

Budget airlines are a perfect example to illustrate the power business models can unfold that are purely focusing on Bargain Customers.

The airline that made budget flying a trend was the American company, Southwest Airlines. Founded in 1967, they became the nail in the coffin for Pan American World Airways (Pan Am). Others had to declare creditor protection. Southwest subsequently became the role model for quite a number of low-cost carriers around the world. In all cases, the established airlines appeared to be caught off guard. Totally unprepared, they were mere passive observers while the budget airlines turned flying into a commodity. If they ever responded, it was always late and often half-heartedly.

In Europe, Ryanair is the budget airline driving the established crazy. The once-small Irish company rapidly became the Nightmare Competitor of the European incumbents. In fact, it is perfect for our detailed Bargain Nightmare Competitor case study. Virgin Blue, Tiger, or other budget airlines provide similar case studies for other parts of the world.

With the knowledge you've already gathered, you should have no problem following us through this case study. If you feel confident enough, give it a go and move ahead on your own. This is the fastest way to learn. It's not important whether you're more familiar with Ryanair or another budget airline. Compare the results later on with what we describe in the following.

The "guided tour" describing the Budget Nightmare Competitor Ryanair relies on the four-step process for Customer-Centric Business Modeling. To make it fun, follow us through the story as we go back to the time when the guys who later founded Ryanair started to think about how they could give the established players the creeps. The Ryanair team didn't have a methodology, of course, to develop Nightmare Competitors systematically at that time. They needed to learn a lot by trial and error. But we can be certain they always wanted to be different and embraced every opportunity to pursue this objective. They certainly would've been extremely grateful for a system designed to make their lives easier.

Imagine being a member of this group and taking part in their session to create a Nightmare Competitor of the established players in the aviation business.

Let's assume the group starts with the observation that all legacy airlines try to address all types of customers. They describe the customers of the incumbents as "people who fly." On this basis, they take the second step and profile the business model used by the established to address these customers. For the profiling, they make use of the Business Model Constituents offering, value-creation system, suppliers, model for utilization, model for generating revenues and standards of integrity.

Regarding the offering, the following observations are collected by the group: all established airlines promise to offer the broadest possible Range of Destinations, around the world if need be on the basis of alliances with other airlines. All airlines offer Frequent Flyer Programs to build customer retention and loyalty. All the established offer different Classes of Travel: economy, business, and first. The collection of offerings is concluded with the observation that all the established are proudly referring to a friendly, far-reaching level of Customer Service.

Next, the value-creation system is on the agenda. The group notes that the incumbents have developed an extensive Infrastructure to Provide Ground Services. Class-related check-in desks and private lounges are part of this infrastructure. It's apparent that all incumbents praise their Planes & the Furnishing of the Planes. Stories to the effect of, "We use this modern aircraft for this route and another for that route and so on" become part of the discussion. And by "furnishing," they mean entertainment systems, modern leather seats, the equipment to cater the different classes, etc.

All participants have seen plenty of marketing campaigns of the aviation's established. They're everywhere but especially in traditional media like print, billboards, and television. The problem is they're all referring to the same flimsy offers. As one of the participants puts it, "Who ever had a good culinary experience of any kind on a plane?" And all group members struggle to keep the ads and campaigns of the different airlines apart.

The last observation has to do with the use of Sales Channels. All the established rely heavily on travel agents. At the same time, they accept bookings from third-party booking engines. Furthermore, they establish direct online ticket sales. So, they're simply making use of all available sales channels.

The suppliers are not seen as crucially important. The group decides not to spend time on assessing them.

Hub & Spoke Systems are identified as the standard model to optimize utilization. The "hub" represents a central airport that flights are routed through, and the spokes are the routes that take the planes out of the hub. The rationale of the established is that by connecting flights, they can maximize the number of passengers per plane.

It's a no-brainer for the group of attackers to integrate Ticket Sales into the profile of the established, as the industry's model for generating revenues.

Finally, the last Business Model Constituent is discussed, but the group struggles to identify special standards of integrity. A discussion about whether safety could be an issue is terminated after a short time. It's hard to operate an airline that isn't taking care of safety. The aviation market is heavily regulated to ensure safety. Therefore, they see safety as a given for any player, new or established.

The findings of the discussion are captured in the Business Model Radar. Since all elements characterizing the business model of the established are seen of high importance to all incumbents, they are positioned at the outer rim of the Business Model Radar. By connecting the dots, the group ends up with the profile of the established airlines. So far, none of the people in this brainstorming session were brought to the limits of their intellectual capacity. They see the exercise as "a piece of cake."

The more difficult part of the process, they expect, is to challenge the model of the established. Some participants have already developed ideas and are impatient to share them. But one group member reminds their colleagues that Step 3 of the four-step process for Customer-Centric Business Modeling is to define the new type of customer.

For the "would-be" attackers, it's no problem. They're a group of penny pinchers creating a business model for penny pinchers. For the attackers, it's clear that customers want to get from A to B for the lowest fares possible. They name the specific type of customers they want to make happy—"People Interested in Budget Travel."

Now, the task at hand is to develop a profile of a

DIAGRAM 7
BUSINESS MODEL RADAR
Established Airline Industry Profile

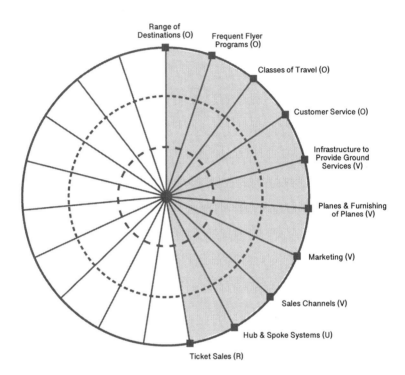

Range of Destinations (O)
Frequent Flyer Programs (O)
Classes of Travel (O)
Customer Service (O)
Infrastructure to Provide Ground Services (V)
Planes & Furnishing of Planes (V)
Marketing (V)
Sales Channels (V)
Hub & Spoke Systems (U)
Ticket Sales (R)

■ **Established Airlines**
CUSTOMER: People Who Fly

Low Importance – – – –	Offering (O)
Medium Importance – – – – – –	Value-Creation System (V)
High Importance ▬▬▬	Suppliers (S)
	Model for Utilisation (U)
	Model for Generating Revenues (R)
	Standards of Integrity (I)

business model designed solely for people interested in Budget Travel. The core offering always has to be stated first. It almost needs no explanation that the core offering of these attackers is Low Fares. After target customers and core offerings are defined, the attackers question which elements of the given business model are relevant to them.

The Range of Destinations, which is so important for the established, isn't an issue. An attacker can't start with the full scope of an incumbent and, why should they? The would-be Nightmare Competitors think about which routes are the most profitable. They decide to follow the cherry-picking approach.

When it comes to Frequent Flyer Programs, they ask themselves whether they even need to discuss the topic. The Flight Categories are immediately ruled out, as well. Why should a new player focusing solely on people who are interested in budget travel have business and first-class? Even the economy class of the established isn't economic enough for the attackers. At this point, they ask themselves why they should even bother to give their single-flight class a name. And nobody sees a reason for doing so. They go on to question why Customer Service, which is basically nonexistent, and certainly unexpected by these target customers, ought to be a topic? Once again, they decide not to bother.

For the industry outsiders, the discussion about Infrastructure to Provide Ground Services and the Planes & Furnishing of Planes is resolved equally fast. "As little as possible" needs to be the motto. They decide to neglect Marketing as much as possible. Who needs marketing when the offering will be a kind of revelation for the target customers? Word of mouth will do most of the work. And because of the presumably magnetic pull, their offering will certainly have the attackers confident enough to provide the customers with just one Sales Channel for purchasing tickets: the company's own website. Nobody is ready to let greedy travel agents participate. They see it as their mission to prohibit such nonsense. The cherry-picking approach in defining which routes to serve makes the Hub-and-Spoke system impractical. What's to connect when there is nothing that can be connected?

One of the most radical of the misers has an especially bright moment and asks his compatriots if they would even be able to offer flights for "free" one day? He introduces the group to the idea of earning the money via the associated services we've already discussed when we introduced the model for generating revenues as a Business Model Constituent. Everyone agrees to the genius of the idea and they agree further that they should become as independent as possible from Ticket Sales.

All elements of the business model of the established have been challenged by now. The group goes back to the Business Model Radar and positions their dots for all the elements the established regard as crucial.

The group is happy with the result. There's hardly

any overlap. They congratulate themselves, because what they've just done is the most difficult job for the established: to kill their own darlings. But as newcomers, they have no problem with killing the darlings of others. So now, it's about coming up with new elements for their own business model.

Someone asks if they could use Regional Airports and develop them into a part of the offering, pointing out that their customers would appreciate it because parking is cheaper than at the main airports, and it would be absurd to ask customers to spend more on parking than on flying. For many customers outside of metropolitan areas, they would even be closer to the airport for a change.

Regional airports, another group member explains, would allow them to be more "on time." Planes wouldn't need to queue up to get permission to take off or land. Usually, there are no other planes. This bonus really excites the group of thinkers. On-time Service is so important that they decide to make it an element of their offerings.

Then the brainstorming almost gets out of control. What about using only a Single Type of Aircraft? The complexity of the value-creation system could be reduced significantly. Costs for maintenance, spare parts, and training could be significantly brought down. Logistical practicalities at the terminal aprons could be reduced and fleet interchangeability increased; both of which could provide further cost reductions. Finally, it's about reducing the purchasing cost.

New planes could be ordered in bulk. The single type of aircraft, of course, influences the supplier relationship, as well. But to keep things simple, they refrain from naming the same aspect twice under the heading of two different Business Model Constituents.

Instead of using a hub-and-spoke system, they discuss a Point-to-Point System. It would provide the equivalent of a bus shuttle service. There would be no delays waiting for connecting flights to arrive. This means short turnaround times and more passengers per aircraft, which in turn, leads to greater efficiency and, therefore, lower costs for the airline while further reducing waiting times for the passengers.

The model to generate revenues returns to the agenda once again. A regional airport playing host to a low-cost carrier means increased revenues for the entire area. Those who benefit could be asked to show their gratitude. They agree, the beneficiaries will be asked for a contribution. And in a similar vein, they discuss deriving a commission-style income stream from Third-Party Revenues, such as car-hire companies, accommodation providers, and travel insurers. Furthermore, they develop ideas for Up-selling Optional Services, among those with potential: checked-in baggage, seat selection, early boarding, or the so-called inflight "food."

Standards of integrity is the last of the Business Model Constituents and isn't a matter of dispute. It doesn't even occur to these people this might be the subject of a debate.

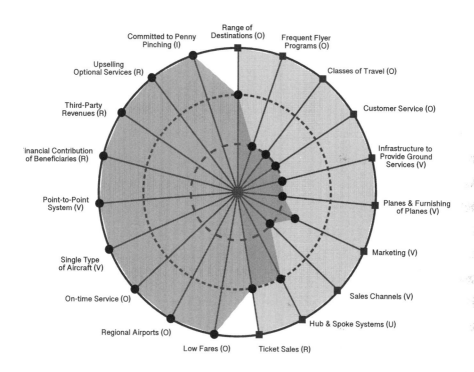

DIAGRAM 8
BUSINESS MODEL RADAR
Ryanair vs. Established Airlines

Range of Destinations (O)
Committed to Penny Pinching (I)
Frequent Flyer Programs (O)
Upselling Optional Services (R)
Classes of Travel (O)
Third-Party Revenues (R)
Customer Service (O)
Financial Contribution of Beneficiaries (R)
Infrastructure to Provide Ground Services (V)
Point-to-Point System (V)
Planes & Furnishing of Planes (V)
Single Type of Aircraft (V)
Marketing (V)
On-time Service (O)
Sales Channels (V)
Regional Airports (O)
Hub & Spoke Systems (U)
Low Fares (O)
Ticket Sales (R)

● **Ryanair**
  CUSTOMER: People Interested in Budget Travel

■ **Established Airlines**
  CUSTOMER: People Who Fly

Low Importance — — —	Offering (O)
Medium Importance — — — — —	Value-Creation System (V)
High Importance ▬▬▬▬	Suppliers (S)
	Model for Utilisation (U)
	Model for Generating Revenues (R)
	Standards of Integrity (I)

After all, they're on a singular mission: they're all totally Committed to Penny Pinching.

After positioning and connecting the dots for the new elements of their value-creation system, they're certain to become the Nightmare Competitor of the European flag carriers.

Indeed, Ryanair found its way. At the time of this writing, it is the largest European airline in terms of scheduled passengers and has carried more passengers than any other airline. It is also one of the most profitable European airline as, in the same reporting year, they posted profits in excess of $1 billion USD after taxes.

Many other Bargain Nightmare Competitors are renowned for their high profitability. Ikea's Ingvar Kamprad and the Aldi brothers made it to the top ranks of Forbes' list of wealthiest people in the world. SpaceX certainly has the potential to be highly profitable. The argument of the established that budget offerings are not attractive because they're not as profitable, is one of the greatest myths of management.

Bargain Nightmare Competitors can be extremely powerful but are still not the most exotic of the Attacker Archetypes. In the following section, we're going to investigate even more revolutionary types of Nightmare Competitors.

The Choice Nightmare Competitor

To keep customers devoted, companies invest heavily in marketing. Powerful brands are created to refrain their customers from looking left or right. Loyalty programs are designed to retain customers even when a company is not able to provide the best offering. Nespresso and Apple demonstrate with their proprietary systems how beautiful it can be for companies to imprison customers within such a kind of microcosm. Taking these efforts into account, it's easy to understand there's one thing the marketing geniuses in particular, and companies in general, can't stand, and that's when offers become comparable.

The idea that their offering could be placed directly alongside that of another company is almost repulsive to them. The idea that features and prices could be directly compared gives them the creeps. Rating systems showing evaluations from customers publicly can raise blood pressures to dangerous levels.

The greatest pleasure for the Choice Nightmare Competitor is to provide everything that the established hate. And unlike the rest of the Attacker Archetypes we've discussed so far, Choice Nightmare Competitors usually don't offer their own products or services. Therefore, they aren't often perceived as competitors by those producing the offerings. However, if a third-party becomes the first point of contact for the producer's customers, what else would we call them? When the established become dependent on the referrals of a new player, what would we call them? When price pressure is increasing because of the transparency that's provided, what else would we call them?

Instead of a competitor, we could of course call them a Nightmare Competitor. This type of competitor is especially nightmarish because the customers are so out of scope. With the Internet becoming a mass phenomenon, most customers started to see total transparency of all offerings and their respective prices as a part of their fundamental right. However, for the reasons mentioned above, the established refrain from granting them what they perceive as a fundamental right, even though each member of their organization is exercising their fundamental right in their role as consumers. The established are not even bothered by the fact that in their mission or value statements, most have stated they'll do whatever it takes to make customers happy. This logic is hard to follow. Barring customers from what they've come to expect leaves the door wide open for attackers.

For potential investors, especially venture capitalists, the Choice Nightmare Competitor is the most alluring of the Attacker Archetypes. There are four very good reasons for this. First, it doesn't take much to establish a Choice Nightmare Competitor. In most cases, we're talking about digital platforms. High schoolers with programming skills can get it done. There's no requirement for a heavy investment in assets, nor in developing the expertise and competences of the established. Second, it's usually very easy to scale up the business, and it's not a problem to expand into adjacent categories. Third, once established, network effects kick in and the platform is hard to displace. Last, it's rather easy to add further services.

Because of these favorable factors, we find Choice Nightmare Competitors in many industries right now. Their offerings range from accommodations, flight reservations, new and used cars, repairs, insurance, music, finance, art, electronics, electricity, legal services, medical services, food, fashion, chauffeur services, steel trading, construction equipment, and the list goes on. Whether B2C or B2B, the Nightmare Competitors make no distinction.

We took great care when choosing the case study for the Choice Nightmare Competitor. For one thing, it's a B2B case study. We want to prove that our Customer-Centric Business Modeling approach can be applied regardless of the boundary between B2C and B2B. The other reason is that it shows that companies establishing products or services in the first place are not the only ones threatened. The case study shows that even traders with an enormously broad scope of offerings can be endangered by Choice Nightmare Competitors.

Nuts-and-bolts items like dowels, screws, zip-ties, drills, drill bits, saw blades, grinding wheels, coatings, and lubricants are typically called "C items." They are relatively inexpensive; hence, they are not A or B items that are managed with greater attention. Related tools, such as screwdrivers and pliers, are also often seen as C items. C items wear out, get lost, and need to be replaced frequently. The trendier term for C items is "MRO articles." "M" stands for Maintenance, "R" for Repair, and "O" for Operations. A whole industry is taking care of providing MRO items.

Companies such as Berner and Würth are well-known players in Europe. With about $10 billion USD turnover, an American company called Grainger is playing in the same league as Würth. This industry sees management's categorizations of their items as a virtue, as nobody else is taking real care of the C items. However, the MRO items are crucial, because in practice, nothing actually happens without their availability: no pipe, no machine, no anything will be mounted if the nuts and bolts aren't available. So, the job of the suppliers of MRO articles is to make the items available where they are needed: construction sites, garages, and wherever you find tradespeople.

Wouldn't it be fun to play the Nightmare Competitor creation game again, this time as a Choice Nightmare Competitor? Put yourself in the position of an attacker and use the four-step process for Customer-Centric Business Modeling to create the most formidable Nightmare Competitor.

We've already described the customers of the industry, haven't we? They're all types of Tradespeople. Therefore,

Step 1 is already done. How would an outsider take care of Step 2 and describe the business model of the industry? What type of customers would the outsider address in Step 3? And the most interesting question needs to be answered in Step 4: which business model would an outsider use to enter the industry?

Let's begin by taking a closer look at Step 2, the profiling of the business model of the established. An Internet search is always a good starting point. It's amazing what can be gathered by surfing websites and simply noting what each of them refer to. Another smart move is to talk to tradespeople regularly buying from the incumbents or talk to a few industry experts. The outsider would be amazed at just how little it takes to describe the business model of Würth, Grainger, and all other suppliers of MRO articles. Systematically following the Business Model Constituents, the outsider ends up with the information noted below.

The established all cover a wide range of trades. So, they basically offer Products for Each Trade. The sales videos on the websites of the established show proud and capable tradespeople. It quickly becomes apparent that only the best will be good enough for these heroes. The quality of the products is conveyed via strong Private Labels. The tradespeople are depicted as tirelessly working against both the elements and the clock. Broken machines need to be brought back online while customers wait desperately for jobs to be completed, and so on.

The requirements on any particular construction project, however, can't always be foreseen. So, Twenty-Four-Hour Delivery/Direct Pickup is another important offering. Some even go above and beyond that. They offer direct pick-up of items in their outlets. However, the established all offer On-site Application Support. They provide comprehensive advice about how to master certain tasks and aren't shy about touting the advantages of using the latest gadgets. The outsider might be happy with the description of the offerings and be ready to move on to the value-creation system.

The backbone of traditional MRO item suppliers appears to be their gigantic Sales Forces. The numbers amaze the outsider. The Würth website boasts incredible numbers. In Germany alone, Würth employs 3,000 sales reps. The majority of their more than 70,000 international employees obviously work in sales. The salesforce visits tradespeople on a very frequent basis. The outsider notices, however, that the terminology is not 100 percent consistent. The customers heap a lot of praise on the personal level of application knowledge and support. So, maybe the sales reps should instead be called "consultants?" The outsider will keep this inconsistency in mind. The sales reps are generally flanked by call centers and websites, from which to order online.

Not all of the industry players seem to place the same value on Outlets. In certain countries, such as Australia, it's almost impossible to establish a tight-knit network of

Outlets anyway. The outsider acknowledges that tradespeople appreciate speedy delivery. However, the outsider is also aware of the investments necessary to establish such Outlets. The established all seem to have an additional Key Account Management system in place. Customers who reach a certain level of business volume, and who have multiple branches, or are considered strategically important for other reasons, are served separately by it.

One thing takes a bit of time to sink in. But there seems to be a guiding principle behind the way in which the established organize their sales process. It's the stories of the tradespeople making fun of the sales reps who grew up carrying around thick, detailed paper Catalogs that let the synapsis connect. These catalogs were the bibles for what is offered, and they contain order codes and list prices. The catalogs are now often substituted by digital ones. But the principle of catalog-based sales still lives on. Updates regarding the set of offerings are made in predefined intervals. And the catalog logic still seems to be the basis for all sales, independent of the channel used. The attacker, therefore, notes the Catalog-Based Sales Process as a further element of the value-creation process of the established.

Another means of lending support and ensuring customer loyalty is the provision of Shelving and Inventory Management Solutions. They're designed for tradespeople who are usually stationary, e.g., car mechanics. These tradespeople simply need or want to have the MRO items available.

The identification of the model to generate revenues appears to be a no-brainer. It's about selling as many products as possible. However, the industry experts and some experienced clients tell the outsider there's a science to the selling process. Sales reps are given extremely ambitious sales targets, and many players seem to provide them with two instruments to foster sales. The first instrument is merchandising to gratify loyalty. The second is a broad flexibility to grant rebates. With these two instruments, the sales reps can adjust to specific customer types. Tough customers are given more attractive deals. The rather ugly side of the story is that the Product Sales with Customer-Specific Incentives usually comes at a cost for the sales reps. Whenever they give sales incentives, their provision is reduced respectively. So, they sell very aggressively, which some customers don't particularly appreciate. Some even claim they're reluctant to open their doors to sales reps, whom they perceive as impertinent.

The outsider might reflect on what they've gathered. The offering has been described well.

The same is true for the second Business Model Constituent, the value-creation system. Suppliers were not an issue. All the incumbents seem to be sourcing from a worldwide network of suppliers and don't appear to be dependent on any of them. So, it's okay not to have a separate element for the suppliers.

The mechanisms to foster sales, discussed under the constituent model for generating revenue, are also

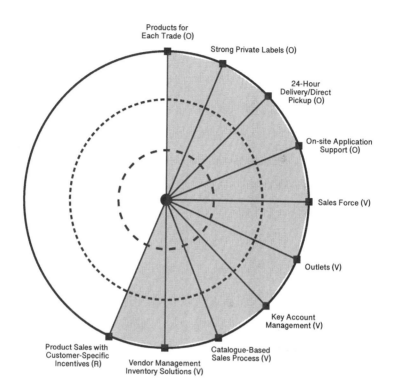

DIAGRAM 9
BUSINESS MODEL RADAR
Suppliers of MRO Articles

Products for Each Trade (O)
Strong Private Labels (O)
24-Hour Delivery/Direct Pickup (O)
On-site Application Support (O)
Sales Force (V)
Outlets (V)
Key Account Management (V)
Catalogue-Based Sales Process (V)
Vendor Management Inventory Solutions (V)
Product Sales with Customer-Specific Incentives (R)

■ Suppliers of MRO Articles
CUSTOMER: Tradespeople

Low Importance	– – –
Medium Importance	– – – – –
High Importance	——

Offering (O)
Value-Creation System (V)
Suppliers (S)
Model for Utilisation (U)
Model for Generating Revenues (R)
Standards of Integrity (I)

supporting utilization. Therefore, there is no need to have an extra item for utilization. The same is true for standards of integrity. The outsider wouldn't be able to identify anything special with regard to this constituent.

So, now it's about time to display the findings in the Business Model Radar. All elements characterizing the business model of the established are seen as important by *all* incumbents. Therefore, once again, they're positioned at the outer rim of the Business Model Radar. By connecting the dots, the group ends up with a clear profile of the industry. This profile is displayed in.

In this case, there's a real company out there that has indeed analyzed the incumbents carefully. The company is an outsider to the industry, but is well-known, nevertheless. Its name is Amazon. To serve the B2B market, they launched Amazon Business in 2015 in the U.S. Subsequent launches in other markets have followed. The objective is to secure a significant piece of the $7 trillion USD B2B sector. Amazon didn't transfer their B2C model directly into the B2B world. The business model needed to be different. Going through Steps 3 and 4 of our Customer-Centric Business Modeling, these differences will show up. You'll also see why Amazon Business will be as nightmarish for the MRO item industry as Amazon has been for B2C retail.

As all Nightmare Competitors do, Amazon thought creatively about which customer they wanted to serve. In times of big data analysis and extremely capable enterprise resource-management systems, the logic behind the ABC analysis appears antiquated. Today, it's possible to manage MRO items professionally, as well. MRO items remain one of the few categories that still offer potential for savings. However, it's not just larger companies that can benefit. Lots of small trades also have an interest in becoming more efficient. For companies, no matter how big or small, Amazon wants to provide the best business model. Therefore, Amazon Business sees its customers simply as, "companies employing tradespeople."

Having defined the customer of the Nightmare Competitor, Step 3 is complete and Step 4 can be addressed. What is Amazon Business already providing or soon to be providing for more of its target customers in other countries?

Amazon's core offering is a Pure Online Procurement System. A company might expect their employees or groups of employees to buy a certain brand of products, or a certain level of quality. If the company has a clear opinion about it, there is no sense in offering options. An access authorization system provides companies employing tradespeople with the opportunity to significantly impact purchase decisions. And it doesn't seem like too much to ask that employees make the purchases online. Most of the employees use Amazon for private shopping, anyway. So, they're capable of ordering online, and they'll be familiar with the look and feel of the provider's functionalities right away. It's somehow taken for granted that Amazon Business is selling solely online and that it's possible to integrate its service into Enterprise Resource Programs.

Having developed an understanding of the core offering, it's possible to think about which elements of the business model of the established are relevant to Amazon Business. Amazon Business might not have all Products for Each Trade available yet. In the beginning especially, established players will have highly specialized products they're not willing to sell via Amazon Business. But this problem will resolve over time. Eventually, at least some established players will start to sell via Amazon Business. After all, Amazon's platform is an open marketplace.

Amazon has been experimenting with Private Labels in its marketplace for consumers. But we could not find any Private Labels on Amazon Business. When entering a new category, it surely isn't their priority to have Private Labels. Interestingly, at the time of writing this book, Amazon Business doesn't meet the same Twenty-Four-Hour Delivery promise that the established offer. Amazon Business currently promises forty-eight-hour delivery. It's easy to imagine, however, that Amazon will soon generate sufficient momentum to hone their promise to that of the established. Direct Pick-up will not be offered. As discussed, Amazon Business is solely an online procurement system.

A company providing a pure online platform and that's also presenting third-party products won't and can't offer On-Site Application Support.

What about the value-creation system?

It didn't require the Forrester Research's study, tellingly titled, "Death of a B2B Salesmen" to inspire Amazon. By default, Amazon Business doesn't need or want a Sales Force. Neither does Amazon Business show any intention to open up Outlets. Like with private labels, this might become an issue when Amazon Business has reached a market dominating position in the online business. With Key Account Management, it's a different story right away. After all, Amazon Business is targeting companies. But the Key Account Managers are supposed to work mainly from their desks and will call their customers.

For Amazon, following a Catalog-Based Sales approach would be like living in a cave. The company has an unparalleled ability to learn from permanent updates of the systems and changes of the products being sold.

Amazon doesn't and won't offer Vendor Management Inventory Solutions. Without their own standardized private-label products, it's not possible to build up proprietary systems. Amazon is aware that users can get such systems elsewhere and most of them have systems in place for the A and B items anyway. For most of these customers, there's no sense of having separate systems for C items.

Neither would Amazon be interested in Product Sales with Customer-Specific Incentives. There are no sales reps out there who could provide the incentives.

Without even connecting any dots, it becomes apparent

that Amazon Business isn't interested in playing the game according to the rules of the established. But what are the new rules of the game Amazon is introducing? The core offering has already been described. But Amazon's new business model has more appealing aspects to offer.

Being a Choice Nightmare Competitor, Amazon Business has to, and of course, does provide Price Transparency. What you see is what you get. The price listed is the price the customer has to pay. There might be rebate levels in accordance with the total turnover a company makes with Amazon Business, but such levels can be communicated openly. The discounts given then apply to all products a company purchases and aren't subject to individual negotiations. Amazon also gives customers more Choice. No matter what brand we're talking about, if something is for sale in a given country, the chances are extremely high that Amazon will offer access to such items. Some customers will want to buy at the lower end of the spectrum because their requirements regarding quality aren't especially high. Of course, others will want the best of the best. Amazon embraces them all. Customers can also see what stock is on hand and in what quantity.

The online platform also provides the opportunity to capture Ratings and Reviews. Reviews and tutorial videos of other users might be even more important in a B2B setting than in a B2C world. In any case, they're better than polished marketing gibberish.

DIAGRAM 10

BUSINESS MODEL RADAR
Amazon Business vs.
Established MRO Suppliers

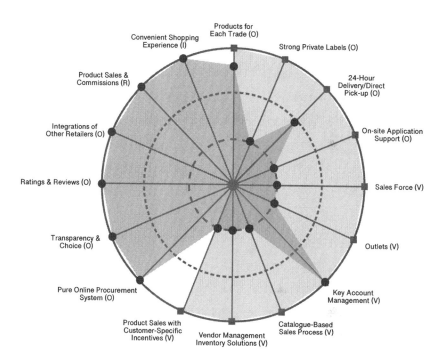

Products for Each Trade (O)
Convenient Shopping Experience (I)
Strong Private Labels (O)
Product Sales & Commissions (R)
24-Hour Delivery/Direct Pick-up (O)
Integrations of Other Retailers (O)
On-site Application Support (O)
Ratings & Reviews (O)
Sales Force (V)
Transparency & Choice (O)
Outlets (V)
Pure Online Procurement System (O)
Key Account Management (V)
Product Sales with Customer-Specific Incentives (V)
Vendor Management Inventory Solutions (V)
Catalogue-Based Sales Process (V)

● **Amazon Business**
CUSTOMER: Companies Employing Tradespeople

■ **Suppliers of MRO Articles**
CUSTOMER: Tradespeople

Low Importance	- - - -
Medium Importance	- - - - -
High Importance	————

Offering (O)
Value-Creation System (V)
Suppliers (S)
Model for Utilisation (U)
Model for Generating Revenues (R)
Standards of Integrity (I)

It's not always the case that a Choice Nightmare Competitor stocks its own items. Think of the many platforms that simply route users to the specific product or service in demand. Amazon itself is a retailer and stocks items. However, they combine both approaches and also route customers to other retailers. The Integration of Other Retailers by giving them the chance to have their own shops within the digital platform is another fundamental aspect. Because of this, Amazon is keeping the transparency promise.

The integration of other retailers enables Amazon Business to also make money via providing the platform. So, the model for generating revenues is expanded, and Product Sales and Commissions can be noted for the profiling.

Does Amazon Business have standards of integrity? Especially in B2C environments, users are concerned about privacy; the insights the company is getting into their private sphere when they shop. On the other hand, users appreciate the quality of the recommendations Amazon can provide based on the insights they gather. With Amazon Business, privacy is less of an issue. Companies tend to be less sensitive than individuals. Anyhow, the important thing when it comes to standards of integrity is whether the company is consistent in what they say and do with customers and stakeholders. Amazon leaves no doubt they utilize user data to provide the most Convenient Shopping Experience in the B2C and, by now, also in the B2B worlds.

After having positioned and connected the dots for

Amazon's business model, it becomes apparent the company does indeed have the potential to turn the market of B2B MRO item trading upside down, just as much as it has shaken up retail. The cost savings of their business model are simply enormous. At the same time, they offer advantages the established struggle to offer. Even if they try to copy Amazon regarding the new elements of their business model, and they're in the process of doing this, the compromises required to bring the traditional business model in line with the new model are simply too substantial. It won't work. The chances are high that the traditional players will become suppliers to Amazon's platform, which of course is fine with Amazon. First, Amazon doesn't want to compete on the basis of their degree of specialization in the product offerings. They want others to take care of the complexity associated with it. Second, they'll be able to define the margins, the more the platform also becomes the standard place to purchase for the majority of companies.

Amazon Business didn't appear from out of the blue, and neither do other portals offering a complete overview of available options, which provide complete price transparency. More companies should strive for Intellectual Leadership.

The Ultimate Want Nightmare Competitor

Aren't all companies designed to meet customers' wants? We certainly hope so. There are companies devoted to building cars, thereby satisfying the desire for mobility. There are companies devoted to developing the best servers in the world, thereby satisfying the desire to store and process data. There are companies importing, refining, and packaging coffee, thereby satisfying the desire for a drink that will keep customers awake.

All these companies see the product as a means to meet the wants of customers The Ultimate Want Nightmare Competitor, however, isn't focused on the *product*. This Attacker Archetype gains its disruptive powers from thinking the other way around, e.g., "Is the product being provided today the *only* way to satisfy the want? Are personally owned cars really needed to provide mobility? Are cars needed at all to provide mobility?" Sometimes, the Ultimate Want Nightmare Competitor goes even further and raises the question of whether there's a want *behind* the want. "Why do customers want to be mobile?" Some of them might want mobility just to meet the underlying desire to exchange information with others. Here, the Ultimate Nightmare Competitor will explore the question of how else information could be exchanged in a meaningful way.

In short, the Ultimate Want Nightmare Competitor thinks about the customer, then works backwards. The Ultimate Want Nightmare Competitor goes beyond the Unique Value Nightmare Competitors and the Bargain Nightmare Competitors to focus on something more than just providing a substantially different or cheaper product. The Ultimate Want Nightmare Competitor also goes beyond the Choice Nightmare Competitor. This type of Nightmare Competitor provides more than just transparency over the given options.

The Ultimate Want logic is not new. Long-dead American economist and Harvard professor, Theodore Levitt, once famously said, "People don't want to buy a quarter-inch drill, they want a quarter-inch hole." That raises the question: "Why are Nightmare Competitors still gaining their disruptive juice out of it?" Let's move from the hardly nightmarish all the way to the completely creepy, and it will become apparent.

Hardly nightmarish: Car manufacturers investing in car rental companies or built-up mobility services like car2go or DriveNow move from product to want. A company called Dürr is offering the service to paint cars as an alternative to purchasing their painting systems. Therefore, they run painting facilities on the car manufacturers' premises and charge for each car painted according to specs. Kuka, a company renowned for making world-class industry robots, offer the service of welding car bodies for car manufacturers as an alternative to purchasing their robots. In all these examples, companies have moved from selling products to meeting wants. The original products, however, remain crucial for all the offerings. Without them, the service offerings could not be provided.

The fact that established companies have been able to move from *product* to *want* doesn't mean it's easy. Providing a service, as opposed to selling products, requires additional and largely adopted value-creation processes. Sales, therefore, needs to adjust to selling a broader range of offerings. However, companies often fail to establish incentive systems that make selling services as attractive as selling products. The service offerings usually require high upfront investments and the turnover and profits are made over long periods of time. Whenever selling services is not as attractive as selling physical products, the motivation to sell the new offering is limited. Production is afraid that the demand for their products will subside when the products are better utilized. Lower volumes, however, mean lower economies of scale. Finance is not only worried about a reduction in turnover, but it's also questioning whether profits will be as high as in the given model. It's the service provider who owns the assets and has to finance them. When interest rates are low, this is less of a worry, but it's a hurdle nevertheless.

For all these reasons, companies struggle to adjust. The

major motivation for crossing the hurdle is usually peer pressure: "If our competitors have it, we must have it, too." When the service model becomes something of an industry standard, even the most reluctant ones follow. But, if almost all players are providing the same service, then we have, by default, left the realm of nightmarish competition anyway.

Reasonably nightmarish: When the established have a disadvantage compared to outsiders, more nightmarish potential is unleashed. Sometimes, it isn't simply the manufacturers of hardware who are in the best position to provide the ultimate want business model. Amazon needs gigantic computing capacities for its own business. Based on just their own demand, it's creating enormous economies of scale. Therefore, it was no problem to offer cloud computing and storage services to third parties at competitive rates directly from the start; something they did when they launched Amazon Elastic Cloud Compute (Amazon EC2) as part of Amazon Web Services. But Amazon has another advantage: they need enormous surplus capacities for their business over the year-end festive period. They can offer these capacities for the rest of the year for a contribution margin to all those businesses that go slow over the Christmas season. At the time of this writing, Amazon Web Services is reported to have more than 40 percent of the fast-growing cloud-computing market, far ahead of rivals such as Microsoft, Google, and IBM.

Viciously nightmarish: The further away the Ultimate

Want is from what the established are offering, the more dangerous the Ultimate Want Nightmare Competitor becomes. The business of producing and selling solar panels is renowned for being a cutthroat business. Most players aren't profitable. SolarCity started with the idea that customers don't want to buy solar panels, they want to produce their own green energy to be self-sufficient. To facilitate that, SolarCity simply made use of available third-party panels and arranged to lease them to homeowners, so that customers no longer had to lay out a chunk of cash. Once installed, customers could also start saving money from day one.

SolarCity created such high demand for solar panels that they've started to produce their own. By focusing on the want instead of the product, they are now in touch with end consumers and have the volumes to generate significant economies of scale. Both factors must be perceived as viciously nightmarish by mere hardware producers. In 2016, Elon Musk made SolarCity a part of Tesla.

Completely creepy: When the new approach has nothing in common with what the established are doing, the ultimate nightmarish potential is set free. Do people really want to drink coffee, or do they want to stay awake? Most still want to drink coffee, but a sufficient number of people, especially among the younger generation, are simply interested in the kick the caffeine element provides. Why didn't coffee companies offer energy drinks? The question becomes even more inconvenient for the established when we consider the fact that the caffeine needed for energy drinks used to be one of the most important ingredients. Today, caffeine can be produced synthetically, but it was originally derived from the process of decaffeinating coffee.

Consider Wilkinson and Gillette. They freed men from throat-endangering razors. Disposable blades marked a great achievement. Razors originally had only a single blade. Later, a second was added. After that, a pair of heads that could adjust to the contour of the face. Then a grid that would prevent cuts. Next, four blades, even five. Now, razors send out electrical impulses to the skin to make the hair stand up at just the right angle. But how many men actually want to shave? How many scientists do Wilkinson and Gillette employ to find a more fundamental solution to the facial hair-growing issue, thereby, meeting the ultimate want? The most likely answer is none.

A similar story can be told about the evolution of the lawn mower. Who wants to mow lawns? The answer provided by the established is autonomous lawn-mowing robots. The nightmarish approach goes beyond a purely technological answer. What about grass seed that stops growing at three centimeters? How many scientists are employed by the big lawn-mowing manufacturers to offer a solution to satisfy the ultimate want of a significant number of today's customers?

As with the three Attacker Archetypes we've covered so far, we want to demonstrate that Ultimate Want Nightmare

Competitors can be created systematically by using our approach for Customer-Centric Business Modeling. This time, we want to carry you off into the world of music. We're amazed how a small Swedish company could become the Nightmare Competitor of mighty Apple. The company's name, of course, is Spotify. Even though Apple is now providing a similar offering, we can assume that Apple did not introduce Apple Music completely voluntarily. The former leader in innovation, Apple had to pay tribute to the strategy of an even more innovative attacker. This alone qualifies them as a Nightmare Competitor, even if Apple eventually manages to regain control.

We don't have any trouble going back to the year 2005 to imagine a few teens sitting together in a cool bar or club somewhere in Stockholm, listening to funky music and no doubt talking about what was going on in the music scene.

Each member of this group certainly has an iPod and buys music via iTunes. Steve Jobs is their hero. For them, he's changed the world for the better. But one of them raises the question about what the future will bring. Is it possible to imagine that one day a new service will rock the world as much as Apple has rocked their world with iTunes? One of them goes back to Jobs and his seeming desire to challenge the status quo. She knows the words of Apple's "Think Different" campaign by heart and recites them.

"Here's to the crazy ones. The misfits. The rebels. The troublemakers. The round pegs in the square holes. The ones who see things differently. They're not fond of rules. And they have no respect for the status quo. You can quote them, disagree with them, glorify, or vilify them. But the only thing you can't do is ignore them. Because they change things. They push the human race forward. And while some may see them as the crazy ones, we see genius. Because the people who are crazy enough to think they can change the world, are the ones who do."

And then the room goes silent. They decide to be the crazy ones, the misfits, the rebels, the troublemakers, at least on that day, in that club, and in that mood. They say, "Nothing can be wrong with envisioning what could be done."

Enlightened by the "challenging the status quo" debate, they decide to first define the status quo to be able to later challenge each and every aspect of it. For them, the status quo is that Apple allows them and millions of other music lovers around the world to listen to music wherever they want. Addressing, "People Who Want the Convenience of Listening to Music" was Apple's first step.

For them, Apple provided unparalleled offerings, the Choice of Titles, for starters. Customers get access to more music than any record store could ever shelf. The music platform appeals to almost every taste of music, from pop to country, rap, blues, jazz, and classical music. And for those young people, the offering of Single Tracks is just as amazing as the choice of titles. Even though entire albums can still be purchased, this is no longer necessary. And having the chance to enjoy the thirty-second Previews of any song with a view to "Try before you buy" is simply great.

For our group, iTunes stands for even more offerings. The ability to Create Playlists from Purchased Titles is great, and like many customers, they like the Purchase Recommendations via Genius. Isn't it awesome to get musical recommendations based on your own listening preferences?

The value-creation system pretty much circles around iTunes as a Platform for Downloads. One thing is clear: to legally provide a wide range of titles, the Management of Intellectual Property Rights is an indispensable ability.

Apple's Model to Generate Revenues is the all-too-familiar Pay Per Sale. Most members of our group no doubt spend a significant portion of their income purchasing new titles.

Maybe it's asking too much from such a group to be aware of the Business Model Constituents. In a Customer-Centric Business Modeling session where the constituents would've been followed systematically, the constituents, suppliers, utilization, and integrity would also be addressed. But the group did a sufficient job. The suppliers are the music companies like Warner Music or Sony Music, making the music available. The group put Management of Intellectual Property (IP) Rights on its list, which is good enough. They addressed the issue that could also be named under the constituent suppliers out of the perspective of the value-creation system. And of course,

DIAGRAM 11
BUSINESS MODEL RADAR
iTunes Profile

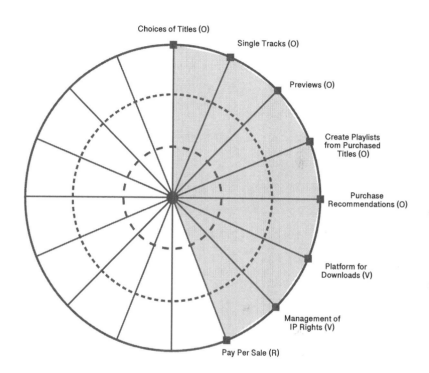

Choices of Titles (O)

Single Tracks (O)

Previews (O)

Create Playlists
from Purchased
Titles (O)

Purchase
Recommendations (O)

Platform for
Downloads (V)

Management of
IP Rights (V)

Pay Per Sale (R)

■ **iTunes**

CUSTOMER: People Who Want the
Convenience of Listening to Music

Low Importance – – – –	
Medium Importance – – – – –	
High Importance ———————	

Offering (O)
Value-Creation System (V)
Suppliers (S)
Model for Utilisation (U)
Model for Generating Revenues (R)
Standards of Integrity (I)

Apple is optimizing utilization by inviting as many users onto the platform as possible. Therefore, this aspect could be part of the status quo description. But this is generic, so maybe there's no harm done in not having it on the list. And as with most incumbents, it's hard to define specific standards of integrity. With Apple at that time, it could've been "challenging the status quo." But the group also wanted to do that, so this element doesn't make a difference.

So, even for a professional creator of Nightmare Competitors, the insights developed by the group are a good starting point. Such a professional would, of course, also have noted all the elements of Apple's business model that were identified in the discussion. This person would have positioned and connected these elements within the Business Model Radar to end up with the profile of the established. For your benefit, we've drawn such a profile.

Let's go back to the club where the group is by now engaged in a deep discussion about how the status quo can be challenged. As apprentices of the great sorcerer Steve Jobs, they decide to follow along the lines of their master. They conclude that he took care of their *real* desire. They always wanted to have their music available anywhere. Buying CDs was never their real desire. But before the messiah showed up, everyone saw the CD as the instrument which allowed people to listen to music. Jobs started from the customer and thought backward, then legalized the idea behind a service that was already out there: Napster. Technology wasn't the issue, and the pirates from Napster had provided the proof of concept.

Thinking backward from the customer, Jobs met the real desires and wants of customers, which resonates with this group of music lovers. So, they ask themselves, "What is it that would rock us?" One of them says, "If I could listen to even more music, that would be great," but with iTunes, this of course costs money, multiple small sums that add up. Someone else is reciting their hymn again saying, "Let's be crazy enough to think we can change the world." They begin to think about what a service to meet their want might look like; a service for "People Who Want to Explore Music."

What would it require to provide happiness for people who want to listen to music? In a perfect world, such a service would offer Free Unlimited Access to Music. Nobody around the table can suppress a smile just thinking about the idea. "That would be nirvana, wouldn't it?" "Smells like teen spirit," somebody replies with a smirk.

They wonder what elements of iTunes could be questioned if they had such an offering? The Choice of Titles? No, the ability to explore music is too critical. When it comes to choice of titles, there's no way to compromise. One option they ponder would be to get rid of certain genres, such as classical music.

In a world of free and unlimited access to music, the concept of selling Single Tracks appears obsolete. And who needs Previews in such a world? The same thing is true of Playlists out of Purchased Titles and Purchase Recommendations. When users already have free access to all titles, the "purchase" concept is no longer applicable. Would a Platform for Downloads still be required? Somehow, downloading doesn't feel right anymore. The group wonders if the concept of *owning* titles is a bit old-fashioned. Wouldn't it be sufficient to simply have *access* to titles? YouTube is already out there. Couldn't music titles just be easily streamed like videos?

The Management of Intellectual Property Rights is an element of the business model where the group sees no chance to challenge the status quo. To have as many titles legally available as possible, IP management is of utmost importance. Pay Per Purchase, however, is part of a system that already feels out of date.

After having challenged all that is holy for the incumbents, the crazy ones are ready to think about adding further new elements to their business model. They start with offerings designed to complement the already-defined core offering.

Users could, of course, Create Playlists out of all titles as track records of their discovery journeys. Even better, it would be possible to Share Own Playlists with Others; a reincarnation of the old mix tape in digital form. How cool! The notion of being able to convey something to friends that might provide them some kicks or drive them out of their melancholy puts smiles on their faces and makes their stomachs turn. They're immediately frenetic fans of this idea.

One of the music enthusiasts wonders aloud whether it might be possible to make playlists public. Access to Playlists of the Crowd would bring thousands of music scouts to the user's disposal. Isn't that great? Even those who listen to "weird" stuff would find their peers, as well as a permanent stream of inspiration. And every "like" and "dislike" of a title would enable them to learn more about the taste of their users. It's also the perfect precondition to provide the best Personalized Radio Stations.

You can imagine everyone high-fiving all around and applauding their own courage. The mavericks are having fun, but what kind of value-creation system would be required to make this offering possible?

Going back to their earlier discussion, the group decides the platform for downloads no longer feels right. They had already discussed the technology behind the recently launched YouTube. They assume music titles can be streamed just as easily and as well as videos. So, they decide that a Platform for Streaming should substitute Apple's platform for downloads.

Talking about the commercial aspects of such a new service, one of the group members has something of an epiphany. The insight she comes up with is as simple as it is convincing. The iTunes model aims to get the maximum return from a single music title from a limited number of users, those who are ready to pay for a specific title. In a new system, it could instead be about utilizing a given title much better. If a much larger number of music lovers would pay a smaller contribution, it could add up to the same amount; long-term, maybe even a larger amount of money. The Utilization of Music, they decide, is key.

The fee could even be covered by others. Apple doesn't allow advertising on iTunes. But wouldn't people be ready to endure advertising if listening to their favorite music were free? For sure! They already listen to poorly compiled music on the radio and endure the most horrible advertising and incessant chatter of radio show hosts. Advertising revenues could definitely provide the financing for the freemium model they have in mind. And the service would be highly attractive to advertisers, as choice of music says a lot about a user. And who could evaluate music taste better than a platform providing free and unlimited access to music? Above all, any of these users could be addressed individually. Magnificent!

The group, drawing on their own experiences, realizes that some sort of Subscription-Based Membership Fee is also a typical element of freemium services. It's part of the model for generating revenues. But what premium services could be offered to justify subscription-based membership fees? Impatient music pros love shuffling. Unlimited shuffling could be reserved for subscribers. A premium, ad-free service could be added that includes the opportunity to download. Willing subscribers would then be able to listen to music in the wilderness regardless of whether or not there's even a signal.

People who are crazy enough to think they can change the world are the ones who do. By this point, they know they can do it. Spotify was subsequently founded in 2006, approximately one year after YouTube. One decade later, Spotify provides access to more than thirty million songs, has 100 million active monthly users in more than sixty countries, and more than fifty million paying subscribers.

By positioning the elements and connecting the dots of the new business model within the Business Model Radar, the business model of the Nightmare Competitor Spotify can be visually brought to life. 2 summarizes the whole story at a glance.

Meanwhile, mighty Apple slept for eight long years before finally responding.

Within eighteen months of launching Apple Music, the company secured twenty million subscribers. Despite Apple's enormous power, many observers give Spotify a good chance to maintain its lead. Its user interface is praised as being more accessible, uncluttered, and having simpler playlist management. Its new music-discovery playlists, especially Discover Weekly, keeps the platform brilliantly fresh, and it's also free for those who aren't willing to commit.

It's amazing that a company long seen as one of the most innovative in the world is struggling so much to fight a startup that's never inhaled Californian air. Apple appears

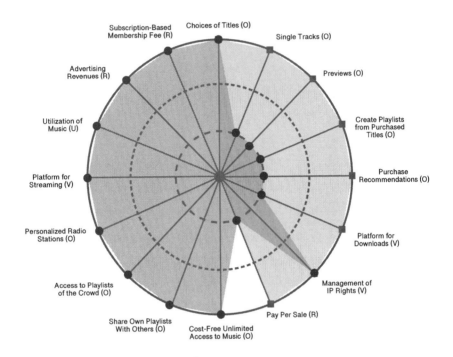

DIAGRAM 12
BUSINESS MODEL RADAR
Spotify vs. iTunes

- **Spotify**
  CUSTOMER: People Who Want to Explore Music
- **iTunes**
  CUSTOMER: People Who Want the
  Convenience of Listening to Music

Low Importance – – –	Offering (O)
Medium Importance – – – – –	Value-Creation System (V)
High Importance ————	Suppliers (S)
	Model for Utilisation (U)
	Model for Generating Revenues (R)
	Standards of Integrity (I)

to be a company clutching to an antiquated business model and taking advantage of its customers for far too long. Don't get us wrong, we don't have a problem with a premium brand charging premium prices for a premium product. But it does need to be a premium product!

Customers noticed how long it took Apple to adjust by launching Apple Music, and that Apple didn't adjust of its own free will. They presumed Apple did it because they were forced to respond to the challenge presented by Spotify. Such realizations act as a catalyst in which customers are able to recall how much they've paid for other Apple products, such as the little adaptors Apple forces its customers to buy. They start to question whether it's a good thing to be imprisoned in a proprietary model such as Apple's. Based on these considerations, it's even possible to bring the standards of integrity into the discussion. But we've refrained from doing so, because this subjective topic might be better left for long evenings in discussion with nerdy friends.

This case study might also provide the established with a sense of hope. It's possible to create the Nightmare Competitor of a Nightmare Competitor. The music industry once developed MusicNet as an answer to Napster but never got it right. A new version of MusicNet could've been the answer to Apple's iTunes. It's a pity somehow that the established have left it up to some Swedish rebels to show the world that Apple is not invincible after all.

The Access Nightmare Competitor

The four Attacker Archetypes described in the previous chapters are Nightmare Competitors in the truest sense. They all provide something to customers that the established aren't. In doing so, Nightmare Competitors are stealing customers away from the established. Unique Value Nightmare Competitors provide bored customers with new kicks. Bargain Nightmare Competitors create the budget offering that sensitive customers are drawn to. Choice Nightmare Competitors make a vast number of offerings available. Ultimate Want Nightmare Competitors provide attractive alternatives for all those customers who never challenged the offering of the established, because they weren't aware there were other options.

Are all potential Nightmare Competitors covered by the four Attacker Archetypes? At first, we thought so, but then realized we have to invite another one into the club—a wolf in sheep's clothing. At first glance, its nightmarish potential is not apparent.

Swiss company Kieser Training is a perfect example of such a hard-to-identify Nightmare Competitor, just as any one of the 150 outlets of Kieser Training might be mistaken for a regular gym to the casual consumer. Through the windows of these modern outlets, observers can see a range of fitness machines. But on closer inspection, many signature traits of the classic gym are missing. There are no scheduled pump or spin classes and no "eight-week challenges." You won't find treadmills, stationary bikes, juice bars, or "wellness treatment centers." They don't even play music. A regular gym? Hardly!

But Kieser doesn't fit into any of the categories of Attacker Archetypes we've introduced so far. As you can imagine, Kieser isn't about providing former gym customers with an even fancier offering. Neither is Kieser offering any form of bargain. Membership fees aren't exorbitant, but taking the basic offering into account, the pricing is rather a testimony of self-confidence. Kieser isn't about Choice. You either choose Kieser or you don't. Full stop. And finally, Kieser hasn't solved the enigma involved in looking fit and healthy without exercising—customers still have to work out. Therefore, Kieser doesn't qualify as an Ultimate Want Nightmare Competitor.

So, what's so special about Kieser? Kieser's specific fusion of physiotherapy with strength and conditioning is designed to help people of all ages manage their chronic pain and avoid surgery. More than 300,000 customers are grateful because they didn't see any of the gyms as an option for them. Some felt too old, too ugly, or too imperfect in some way. Others simply weren't excited by what makes a gym a gym. Kieser is taking care of people who are involuntarily or explicitly shunned by the established.

We found other examples.

When Nintendo introduced the Wii in November 2006, the product could have been mistaken for just another game console. It had to be connected to a monitor, it was about playing games, and the other ubiquities that make a game console a game console. True, the Wii remote controller could be used as a handheld pointing device, and also detect movement in three dimensions, which was something entirely new. Therefore, there is an element of unique value. But it was something the dominant players in the game console market, Microsoft and Sony, could also have invented or copied in no time. While it was somewhat cheaper than Microsoft's Xbox 360 and Sony's PlayStation 3, it definitely wasn't a bargain. It wasn't about choice either. And it certainly wasn't about being entertained by anything other than a video game.

Like Kieser, Nintendo focused its Wii on customers who weren't being addressed by the industry. Microsoft and Sony would've been as likely to market to families as gyms would've been to market to the elderly. The established saw young males as their core audience and tried to outpace each other in the quest for faster, more action-packed, realistic, and better-animated games; games that required incredibly fast processors and the best devices for capturing data. Many families even saw such consoles as a danger to balanced, quality family life. The two parties simply didn't match up.

W. Chan Kim's and Renée Mauborgne's book, *Blue Ocean Strategy: How to Create Uncontested Market Space and Make the Competition Irrelevant* is the ultimate gold mine for such examples. They introduced Pret a Manger, NetJets, Home Depot, and many more companies in their case studies. The title is supposed to make it clear: the market space is uncontested because nobody has ever taken care of these customers before. Therefore, there's no competition, so it's a blue ocean.

Despite our love of the book, we don't concur with the idea that their examples are about uncontested markets completely, nor with the general metaphor of the blue ocean, where nobody has sailed before. In reality, most of the business models Kim and Mauborgne refer to interfere with established businesses. Some mature gamers with families refrained from buying a brand new console in the traditional mold, opting instead for the Wii. Pret a Manger is taking some customers away from other sandwich shops and restaurants. NetJets is taking at least a tiny fraction of customers away from commercial airlines or other transportation companies. And Home Depot is surely taking customers away from traditional hardware stores. In the example we started with, Kieser, some people who used to go to traditional gyms now appreciate the chance to work out in thirty minutes. Let's conclude that the ocean is at least not completely blue.

The competitive element should not be neglected. And as we've already stated, the threat allows you to mobilize much more than the opportunity. Therefore, we recommend staying true to the Nightmare Competitor logic. Companies that invite the apparently odd ones into the realm of the industry and, in the wake of it, deprive the established of cherished customers we call Access Nightmare Competitors.

There's a company out there that introduced a concept for an Access Nightmare Competitor, which gave the established the creeps. That company is Google. And the concept we're talking about is the Google Car Project. Even though Google won't pursue the approach as initially announced, they've inspired a lot of startups. Their plans and activities, as well as Google's revised plans, will certainly have an impact on the incumbents' managers' nightly rest.

It's a perfect case to be discussed based on our methods. What's going on is highly dynamic and the outcome is speculative. By now, you have gathered extensive expertise in developing business models systematically. Let's find out how far we get together. If you find the outcome convincing, you have confirmation that the Customer-Centric Business Modeling not only allows you to analyze the ways of Nightmare Competitors in retrospect, but it also enables you to derive what Nightmare Competitors could be up to. Since the case study is far away from the fantasies of petrol heads, it will be especially appealing to people with no interest in cars.

You've probably seen pictures of Google's "egg on wheels" with a data-collection pimple on top. The pimple in conjunction with advanced software allows for totally autonomous driving. Consequently, the car has no steering wheel, nor does it have brakes or accelerator pedals. Most people struggle to think of it as a real car because of its odd appearance and the lack of components usually seen as crucial elements of a car. Since it has so little to do with a regular car, it's maybe more appropriate to call it a "robocar" instead. Or what about "robocab?" Then, the name does not even include the word "car" anymore. Therefore, maybe it's more appropriate.

The robocab idea doesn't interfere with what Tesla does. Tesla has occupied the Unique Value Nightmare Competitor position perfectly. The affluent green fancy their premium, well-designed, sporty Teslas. Is it about cheaper cars? No, the position of the Bargain Nightmare Competitor is rather occupied by companies like the Romanian car manufacturer, Dacia. Is it about choice? Car-sharing platforms are perfect for offering variety. The Ultimate Want of business people—to be released from the burden of traveling—is satisfied to some degree by new generations of video conferencing. We have already referred to the Double as a great new offering in this realm.

The Google Car Project was designed from the very start to provide access to mobility for people who currently struggle with mobility; but people who would, nevertheless, like to have all the amenities car drivers have. In their videos, Google featured blind and elderly people and kids. They were reaching out to people who don't have the ability to drive or simply feel stressed by today's traffic situation. Thus far, nobody has taken care of this target group, which can be characterized as, "People Who Want to Drive But Can't" as explicitly as Google, with their concept for robocabs.

"People who want to drive but can't" is a marginal group, but in many nightmarish examples we've seen, such laser-sharp focus has an advantage: it prevents the Nightmare Competitors from compromising. In practice, more people usually become part of the customer demography because they appreciate the offering, too. In the case of Google's Car Project, the vast number of people using public transportation also becomes relevant. For them, public transportation might be better than driving a car. Let's face it, public transport is often faster and usually cheaper. But does anybody enjoy public transportation?

The Google approach no doubt provides new customers with access to something the industry hasn't yet offered. But what is the disruptive element that made Google a serious potential Nightmare Competitor? The nightmarish element for the established comes in when you consider everyone who's using their car but hates the endless traffic jams in congested metropolitan areas. The "Ultimate Driving Machine," as coined by BMW, rings painfully while sitting in a traffic jam. *Vorsprung durch Technik* ("Advancement through Technology," an Audi strapline) doesn't help, either. And how much does Mercedes' motto, "The Best or Nothing" alleviate the frustration of a tedious rush-hour commute?

The established rarely stop to consider the less traditional categories of people, whom we discussed above. But, they would be directly affected by people ready to abandon their premium vehicles to hail a robocab with a smartphone. For many drivers tired of traffic jams, the question whether it is still sensible to even own a car will become more and more relevant.

Following the steps of Customer-Centric Business Modeling, let's examine what Google had in mind and what, with variations, will surely become a reality in metropolitan areas around the world.

Steps 1 and 2 can be ticked off in seconds. We've already discussed the customers of the established and the elements of their business model when we introduced Tesla as their Ultimate Want Nightmare Competitor. The profile of the established from this exercise needs to be applicable as a basis for creating any other type of Nightmare Competitor for the automotive industry. Therefore, we simply return to it.

For heterogeneous types of customers, the global automotive industry is offering a wide Range of Models, an enormous spectrum of Features & Engine Concepts, great Design & Prestige, as well as various Purchasing Options. We defined the value-creation process earlier by referring to their Extensive Marketing, their Dealerships, and their role as Orchestrators. With respect to the third Business Model Constituent, suppliers, we referred to their use of Multiple Sources. The instrument to achieve utilization, Economies of Scale, is the volume of cars sold. The Model for Generating Revenues is based on Selling Cars & Financing and After-Sales Service.

Using the (rather extreme) customer definition of "People who want to drive but can't," Step 3 of Customer-Centric Business Modeling is taken care of, and we can take care of Step 4, and begin to describe the ideal business model for the Access Nightmare Competitor.

For the defined target group, one core offering is crucial: Individual Mobility as a Service. Since our target group can't drive, it really needs to be a service. A car-sharing platform would not be good enough. What about Uber or taxis? They provide mobility as a service. To really set the Google Car Project apart, another element was required; not to be dependent on a driver. Therefore, it was necessary to have Autonomously Driving Vehicles. They had to become part of the core offering.

On this basis, which elements of the business model of the established can we question? A wide Range of Models isn't required. Why offer an enormous spectrum of Features & Engine Concepts? Design and Prestige and various Purchasing Options don't need to be part of the offering, either. The value-creation system doesn't require Dealerships. The cars won't be sold or taken to dealers for maintenance. Neither is Marketing required. Can you imagine anyone who won't be talking about this? Would a Nightmare Competitor have an interest in being an Orchestrator and taking care of Multiple Sourcing? Certainly not. Initially, at least, the relatively low volume of cars wouldn't allow them to gain Economies of Scale on the Basis of Car Sold. And the model for generating revenues wouldn't be based on Selling Cars & Financing or on After-Sales Services.

Isn't this extreme? None of the elements of the traditional business model are relevant for the new business model. Enormous amounts of money could be saved, especially by reducing the traditional set of offerings and by dodging the traditional value-creation system.

However, considerable investments are required to provide the value-creation system for the new offering. Autonomously Driving Vehicles are needed. And autonomous driving isn't a piece of cake. Even the tiniest mishaps are likely to draw enormous attention as the first fatal accidents involving Tesla's system have shown. An adequate Car as a Service Infrastructure is the second element of the value-creation system. The cars need to be available, cleaned, charged, and checked.

No such Nightmare Competitor will produce the cars itself; they will rely on suppliers. The attacker will presumably have a Single Supplier just like Apple does for their phones and computers. A supplier like Magna would be perfect. The Austrian company is an expert in producing whole vehicles and has done exactly that for several car brands already. Another option would be to engage a car manufacturer as a supplier. We doubt it would be one of the premium brands. Their self-esteem and high cost structure don't make them the natural partner to team up with. But there are plenty of companies around the world able to produce small cars according to predefined specs.

When not in use, the cars need to be "waiting" somewhere, ready for deployment. However, since the aim is to keep the cars utilized, Availability Management is an indispensable capability. To properly take care of utilization, it makes sense to establish such services in metropolitan areas first.

What about the model to generate revenues? Of course, the Nightmare Competitor can charge for its service per minute or per mile. However, we believe that Data-Based Revenues will be the major source of income. How valuable would it be to repurpose our usual commute time, especially when drivers no longer have to drive? How valuable would it be to know exactly where people are and have an intimate knowledge of their preferences?

The last Business Model Constituent we need to discuss is standards of integrity. Most cars are parked about 95 percent of the time. This only makes sense for car manufacturers whose interest is simply to sell as many cars as possible. From a resource perspective, it's complete cretinism to own such an expensive product you hardly use. In that vein, a small electric motor might do the job just as well as the V-8 on a commute to work. On top of the resources needed to produce a car, resources are spent housing all the idling assets surrounding the car. Imagine being able to repurpose 50 percent of all parking lots? For that matter, what could be done with the land currently occupied by service stations? So, Resource Reduction is something we definitely shouldn't forget in our list of business model elements.

The same process described here can be applied to public transportation, regular mobility services like car2go and DriveNow, as well as Uber's ride service. A business model based on robocabs is the Nightmare Competitor of them all. Uber is the most interesting of these players. Until the idea of robocabs popped up, they were seen as the Nightmare Competitor to all the other players. But consider the cost of having drivers. Think about the greater complexity of orchestrating cohorts of people. Most importantly, think about the inferior revenue model. The consequences of this observation are crystal clear. And Uber understands that.

Uber has launched its own activities in the driverless realm. Following their acquisition of a company called Otto, they created quite a buzz with a self-driving truck they used to deliver 50,000 cans of Budweiser. At first glance, it seems their chances to be the leader of the pack aren't

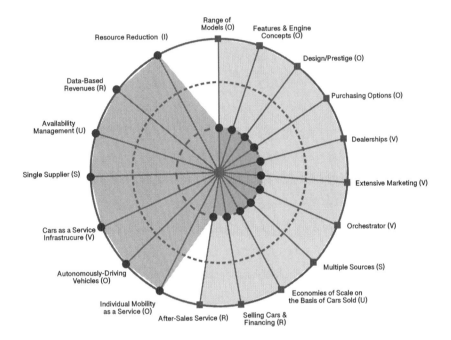

DIAGRAM 13
BUSINESS MODEL RADAR
Robocab vs. Automotive Industry

Range of Models (O)
Features & Engine Concepts (O)
Resource Reduction (I)
Design/Prestige (O)
Data-Based Revenues (R)
Purchasing Options (O)
Availability Management (U)
Dealerships (V)
Single Supplier (S)
Extensive Marketing (V)
Cars as a Service Infrastrucure (V)
Orchestrator (V)
Autonomously-Driving Vehicles (O)
Multiple Sources (S)
Individual Mobility as a Service (O)
Economies of Scale on the Basis of Cars Sold (U)
After-Sales Service (R)
Selling Cars & Financing (R)

● **Robocab**
CUSTOMER: People Who Want to Drive But Can't

■ **Car Manufacturers**
CUSTOMER: Everybody

Low Importance – – –	Offering (O)
Medium Importance – – – – – ·	Value-Creation System (V)
High Importance ———	Suppliers (S)
	Model for Utilisation (U)
	Model for Generating Revenues (R)
	Standards of Integrity (I)

bad at all. The amount of data that can be captured corresponds directly with the miles driven. With all their cars manned with drivers out there, they could gather experience in terms of autonomous driving much faster than Google. And they seem to be determined. They are trying to hire Google's experts and are constantly under scrutiny for making use of Google's intellectual property.

It can be assumed the very same considerations are the reason why Google has abandoned the initial project of launching its own robocab service. The new idea is to provide the relevant software and hardware for autonomous driving to as many players as possible. This way, Google has the chance to gather even more data than Uber and develop its technology faster.

Google has another advantage: who in the world has more experience with data-based revenues? Google will certainly do whatever it takes to be the party in direct contact with the end user. And by connecting what they will be providing to robocab companies and also any car manufacturer that is interested in their current products, they are able to offer an unparalleled range and quality of digital services.

Google will know if we're hungry and provide us with recommendations and vendor-supplied special offers before we even feel the first pang of hunger. They will know we need a new hair dryer and remind us to buy it at the right time. And, of course, you could expect a reminder to buy a gift for an upcoming wedding anniversary or birthday! The possibilities are endless. Sundar Pichai, CEO of Google, probably asked his team, "Do we really need to get our hands dirty and invest gigantic sums of money into a fleet of cars to achieve what we want?" And it seems they concluded they would let others do that.

Taking all this into account, we assume that Google is going to win the game. Reflecting on what Google is up to, it needs to be acknowledged that we're talking about a Nightmare Competitor that relies on technology. This may initially appear contradictory when considering what we stated at the beginning of Chapter 2, where we claimed that Nightmare Competitors usually *don't* rely on technology, but rather, win by making use of business models as their weapon.

Considering what we have discussed in the preceding paragraphs, it's clear to see Google is likely to win the race, because they are brilliant in Customer-Centric Business Modeling. The technology without the business model is not sufficient, no matter how advanced it is; it can be developed by others, too.

In an ultimate scenario, we can even imagine that Google is giving away IT hardware and software for free. Their revenue model, and the reason they are avoiding all associated investments, gives them the chance to go that far. And who could resist such an offering? Google has already gathered significant experience in providing offers that are apparently free. Free, however, is only a service for those who don't consider giving away data as a form of payment.

The four steps of Customer-Centric Business Modeling, the introduction of the five types of customers, and the corresponding archetypes of Nightmare Competitors, as well as the many examples and case studies, should provide you with all the knowledge necessary to attain Intellectual Leadership. However, knowing is one thing; being able to actually rock your own ship is another. In the following chapter, we'll focus on the practical part.

④

ROCKING THE SHIP

The world is in session. Political, economic, social, technological, ecological and environmental factors are changing rapidly. Great times for business innovators. However, the examples and case studies we have discussed in Chapter 3 should have made one thing clear: companies do not need to depend on such external developments. It's possible to be extremely successful in markets that all players consider saturated.

Many of the Nightmare Competitors we've used as examples were not interested in whether markets were saturated or not. Neither did they rely heavily on trend analysis. Many of the trends are so broadly discussed and obvious, that following them alone does not provide any competitive advantage. All the other players in the industry are following them, too. The Nightmare Competitors don't make their strategic decision dependent on outside developments. Rather, they create trends themselves and, thereby, change the world we live in.

Flying to another city for a day of shopping or sightseeing became a trend because budget airlines made it affordable. And wearing a different watch every day became a trend, because Swatch sold watches as fashion items. But let's refrain from going through all the examples again.

How is your company going to change the world, and what is your contribution to it? This is the only question that counts in practical terms.

Most established organizations struggle to convince stakeholders that they see the world as a bonanza of opportunities and that they aspire to change the world. But isn't this exactly what everyone in an organization should be striving for, what all stakeholders are interested in?

Shareholders want to see that there are mavericks at work. They want to hear how the company intends to multiply the share price. Shareholders love to listen to projections of how the company will impact things. If such stories can't be conveyed, they go into "grumpy mode" and ask for dividends and scrutinize quarterly results.

The most capable job applicants want to change the world. They're self-confident and spend great effort to identify a company that offers them the best opportunity to apply their talents to that cause. They're looking for companies that allow them to be mavericks. No matter which "generation label" others want to stick on their backs or foreheads, these guys are ready to work like maniacs when their objectives sync up with their company's. And for many of them, high salaries can't compensate for a lack of meaning.

The most innovative suppliers have the chance to work for a multitude of companies. The more innovative the suppliers are, the greater the choice. Guess which customers they choose? They choose the ones that allow mavericks to prosper. Innovative suppliers can be sure their contribution will be appreciated and that cross-fertilization will give them the chance to become even better. They appreciate, furthermore, that these companies don't have purchasing departments behaving like the descendants of the Spanish Inquisition but instead, strive to build partnerships for the benefit of mutual and rapid development.

Politicians want to ally themselves with those who embark to explore the new. They speculate that some of the positive image the explorers have will be transferred to them. Municipalities and whole regions try to attract the mavericks. They want to claim that their geographical sphere is home to the next Silicon Valley. Therefore, they need to be attractive to forerunners. The companies who are leading the pack have the best chance to benefit from the tokens of friendship which are usually offered to them.

Current employees also gain great value in working

for a company that's permanently questioning and reinventing the assumptive business model of its industry in a customer-centric way. It's the only way they can expect long-term job security.

So, if you work for a utility company, ask yourself what can be done to ignite a broad internal discussion about the possible business models which could go beyond the traditional concepts of large power stations and nationwide high-capacity grids? What could make locally produced energy even more successful? Can you make self-reliant, local energy units a viable alternative? What opportunities will you create on the basis of new technologies like the blockchain? Can you use electric cars as gigantic buffers for electricity? We don't need to scratch more than the surface. You can either see all of this as a threat, or you can try to shape what's going to happen.

If you work for a large telco, what is it you can do to convince the world that you are indeed connecting people regardless of where they're based and that your core competencies go beyond providing poor bandwidth at high prices wrapped in opaque contract models? What do you do to show the world that you'll take care of this as opposed to the Internet companies shooting satellites into orbit out of pure frustration over the inadequacy of communication services in large parts of the world?

If you work for a traditional company within the food sector, do you think about how you can provide more people with better nutrition? Everyone understands that sugar and corn don't comprise a healthy diet, but the alternatives are expensive and often hard to obtain. Don't get us wrong, we aren't advocating vegetarianism or veganism nutrition in a religious way. But obesity has become an epidemic. Doesn't this provide a cosmos of new opportunities? Who will be the one showing that things can be changed on a grand scale and with commercial appeal?

If you work in the media industry, you may, like many other players in the industry, have surrendered to Twitter and Facebook. But what's next after Facebook? Our kids have no interest in using their parents' social media channels. Snapchat and Tinder provide a sample taste. Instead of spending so much time scolding social media for its lack of quality information, or for that matter, fake news, the media might consider rethinking its stance. Tabloids around the world have pioneered the invention of "alternative facts," after all. New business models that would provide reliable content are in high demand. Can you as a journalist rethink what you're currently doing? Questioning the status quo, a hallmark of good journalism, might be a first step.

It's just as easy to come up with similarly inconvenient questions if you work in the health sector, education industry, banking, insurance businesses, and so on. The sector where it's actually easiest to ask inconvenient questions are the professions: tax advisors, doctors, and lawyers rely on legal entry barriers. Their professions are protected. However, are entry barriers really in the best interest of clients? If you're a member of one of these professions, you'll no doubt have learned to argue in favor of such barriers. But what about the hourly-rate pay structure we discussed earlier? If children immediately understand how to manipulate this logic to their favor, then as a representative of one of these fine professions, shouldn't you start to think about it?

One type of profession we haven't yet touched on is the business consultant. Being in a consulting role ourselves we also need to discuss the consultants for us to be credible.

If you are a business consultant, ask yourself what you can do to solve the problem of industry convergence caused by the typical industry white paper approach for acquisition. What can consultants come up with to provide clients with fundamentally unique solutions to set them apart on the basis of business models others don't have access to? What can consultants do to make assignments more affordable? What can consultants do to make customers more self-sustaining? Shouldn't consultants be ready to teach clients the methods they are applying?

As it is becoming apparent, most consulting companies operate spaceships of their own. They, too, work with economies of scale, gathering more and more clients. Their fundamental topic, however, isn't technology. Most consultants operate on the assumption that the only way up in the hierarchies and incentive schemes of their firms is to acquire more and bigger projects. Thus, the more junior consultants and business analysts employed, the better for them. They see repeatable projects as a virtue. But is all this really customer-centric?

We are deeply convinced that consultants need to follow a different approach. It's not about knowing better, it's about enabling. As consultants, we are customer-centric if we help our customers to become Business Model Mavericks. The potential lying dormant in companies is enormous. Our job is to make it accessible.

TURNING MANAGERS INTO BUSINESS MODEL MAVERICKS

Neither top executives nor the consultants they employ can force people to transition from where a company is today to where it wants to be. People are motivated to change when they understand that the transition is necessary and leads to upsides for most stakeholders of the company, themselves included. The more these people are part of the process of developing new opportunities, the easier it is for them to develop the required insights. Being members of such initiatives, they will raise their hand and say, "I'm in, you can count on me."

It's sensible to involve employees for another reason: they provide an incredibly valuable pool of knowledge and competences. The problem is, too many companies have put their employees into a state of mind in which they no longer see much sense in offering their capabilities. The power play taking place in corporate spaceships has deprived them of the desire to stand up. Instead, it is making them rather cautious.

Since we're convinced that managers on a grand scale should be involved in the process of rocking the corporate ships, we define the term "manager" as broadly as possible. In this sense, most people within an organization are managers. This view provides access to more potential and allows the opportunity to create momentum.

There's another reason for involving more people: the only way to permanently adapt is to allow different opinions and provide breeding grounds for them. The arch enemy of reflection and change is synchronization. But if there is one thing the whole discussion of Customer-Centric Business Modeling teaches us, it's that there's no single approach that will make everybody happy. And given the nature of today's world, that's a moving target, anyway.

Imagine what could happen if you familiarized a group of managers with everything we've been describing. The group would see how the need for economies of scale has caused their spaceship to become bigger and bigger. They'd understand that nobody was acting with malintent. Still, they would acknowledge that their spaceship has become too inflexible to master the challenges ahead. Furthermore, they would be aware that their company has become easy prey for predators.

For them, it would be pretty clear the aggressors will use customer-centric business models to launch their attacks. They'd agree they need to assess the potential moves of any Nightmare Competitor that could endanger their industry, and with it, their own business. They'd see the necessity of thinking as radically as possible to be able to determine the future of their industry.

What if you offered them the chance to playfully and virtually attack their own industry to escape the typical planning routines and attain the required Intellectual Leadership? It turns out, people are eager to participate. It's an invitation that restores the gleam in their eyes after feeling hopeless because their initiatives haven't led anywhere.

It's possible to bring managers into this state, and we have made the experience that even groups of very conservative and introverted managers are able to achieve remarkable results. If you want to give it a go yourself, we invite you to apply the tools we introduced in Chapters 1 through 3, and to run your own Rocking the Ship Workshop. To facilitate your workshop, you can also make use of the design we developed over the years and that serves us well when we are invited to conduct workshops.

Start your Rocking the Ship Workshop with questions like, "Why were smartphones not launched by mobile phone companies? Why was drinking coffee not reinvented by traditional coffee companies? Why were budget airlines not invented by the flagship carriers? Why were music companies not offering downloading or streaming? Why was electro-mobility not established by the traditional car industry? Why was solar energy not made successful by traditional utility companies?" These questions will provide you with the opportunity to explain the Corporate Spaceship story and the fundamental idea of the Nightmare Competitors.

This sets the scene for raising more personal, company-related questions like, "How much of your time do you spend in internal meetings a week?" or "On a scale from one to ten, with one representing an inflexible Corporate Spaceship and ten being a pure customer-centric Nightmare Competitor, where would you position our company?" Usually, the consolidated answers speak for themselves and convince everybody that the company is indeed vulnerable.

Based on such a buy-in, the participants are now ready to devote their full attention to learn the methods that will allow them to create the Nightmare Competitors of their industry. In a first step, the participants are made familiar with the Business Model Constituents to describe the business model of their own industry. Several groups can work simultaneously. The groups are asked to present their findings as profiles within Business Model Radars. Usually, their findings overlap greatly, so a "best of" version is created. All that has been described so far does not take longer than half a day. The mix of reflection, introduction of theory, discussions, and practical work makes it an entertaining experience.

The second half of the day begins by introducing the group to the process of Customer-Centric Business Modeling and the Attacker Archetypes. Then, the participants are once again split into subgroups. Each of the subgroups has to attack their company's industry from a different angle. They are expected to transfer their findings into profiles for the Nightmare Competitor and to match this profile with the consolidated profile of the industry.

To meet their task within a relatively short time budget, the groups need to work in "Angel's Advocate" mode. The method is also known as "creative enforcement." It ensures that the groups will not waste time on evaluating ideas too early when they have not yet unfolded their full beauty. The members of the group are not supposed to discuss, but rather, advance all possible ideas that might support the first one. As the name suggests, they become Angel's Advocates. This way, rapid prototyping becomes possible. Devil's advocates are not wanted.

Officially, the first workshop day ends with the creation of the Nightmare Competitors, but as you can easily imagine, the exercise doesn't leave anybody cold. And the insights the groups have derived will provide the basis for discussions among participants, which often lead well into the small hours of the morning.

The next morning, the groups present the Nightmare Competitors of their own industry. The atmosphere is lively. The flipcharts with the results are still spread all over the place, and everyone listens to the explanations of each group's spokesperson. A rigid time schedule for the presentations provides no room for lengthy debates. Only clarifying questions are allowed. It's fun to see how eager the groups are to convince the others that the attacker they have created is the creepiest.

Then, each participant of the workshop receives five "coins" representing $500,000 USD or some equivalent in local currency to invest into the Nightmare Competitors. They should assume the money is a fair percentage of their savings. And there is only one rule to follow: they are not allowed to invest more than $200,000 USD, two of their five coins, into their own business model. It's amazing how fast the investment game can make the nightmarish potential of the various potential attacks apparent. And there's no going back and forth. The discussion finally taking place at the end of this step usually centers around explaining *why* some of the business models got all the money.

The afternoon of the second workshop day is used to talk about the implications; what should the company do on the basis of the new insights? In the following chapter, we'll provide further input for this discussion.

The typical feedback after such a two-day event is, "If anybody had told us two days ago what astounding results can be achieved within such a short span of time, we would not have believed it." The participants also realize with awe that they have somehow turned into Business Model

Mavericks. It won't be possible to forget what has been discussed. And there are many others sharing the same insight. Going back to the daily routines doesn't feel right anymore.

Anyone who wants to run their own Rocking the Ship Workshop will also be interested in the video tutorials, templates, and other materials we provide at our website: *www.rockingtheship.com/bookresources*

It's possible to run workshops with groups composed of between twelve and forty people. An ideal size is twenty-five people. This makes it possible to simultaneously run five subgroups of five people each. Throughout the workshop, we put great effort in mixing groups by defining new group constellations. This makes sure the effort is as much a joint effort as possible.

A lever for developing the maximum momentum is to run several Rocking the Ship Workshops independently from each other. And if you can, base them in different parts of the world. The greater the number of events, and the more heterogeneous the participants, the greater the spectrum of approaches. More ideas of what can shape the future of the industry will be at your disposal.

If you run Rocking the Ship workshops, consider capturing the entire event with a professional camera team. Camera teams are usually quite good at blending into the background. In minutes, people seem to forget the team is even there. This way, you can create sizzle reels to excite the rest of the organization. They provide a glimpse into the group dynamics and displays the contagious enthusiasm of the participants. Of course, the filming also allows you to nicely capture the workshop outcomes.

When top management asks us to facilitate workshops, we recommend they stay out of the process. Of course, this depends on personalities, size of the organization, corporate culture, and other aspects. However, the beauty of it is that after having carried out a workshop successfully, top management doesn't need to preach the necessity of change any longer. Top management only needs to be open for radical suggestions and to foster the momentum created.

Workshops can be initiated and carried out by anyone within an organization. Members of strategy or marketing departments, for instance, almost by definition need to be interested in new methods allowing their companies to develop new business ideas and models. However, we also see a rising demand from corporate departments like legal or HR for developing their Nightmare Competitors. Whenever the results of such workshops are presented to higher levels of management, the presenters are the ones who need to take care that the managers they address are made familiar with the philosophy behind the approach and the method itself.

THE MAVERICKS MATRIX

Let's assume your company's Rocking the Ship Workshops have led to important results. Despite everyone's enthusiasm, we all know from experience that the process of transferring new business ideas into actual business activities usually takes time—a lot of time. And often, the new ideas are appreciated, but perceived as a bit too extreme. So, they get watered down. The compromise reflex is simply too powerful.

That's not good enough. Companies run a great risk by waiting or negating the extreme elements of new business models. And, it is demotivating all those beneath the top management level who invested their time and energy in the workshops.

We created the Mavericks Matrix to remind every member of an organization just how important it is to be fast and to be bold. As you might expect, the Mavericks Matrix is defined by the two axes: speed and boldness.

Let's stress why the first axis, the one dealing with the necessity to stay ahead is important.

Often, the established give Nightmare Competitors enough time to occupy the market. At first, only a few customers begin to feel understood by and comfortable with the outsider. But after being positively surprised, some even become ambassadors for the new player. The opinion leaders start to describe the established as the "old guard." More people begin to see that the outsider is actually providing an interesting offer. They start to talk about the differences in the business models of the newcomers and the established.

The media picks up the topic. The extent to which they like such stories is something that can be easily observed at the moment. It seems difficult to sell a business magazine without the face of an industry outsider giving established players a hard time on the cover. And if it isn't Musk, it's Daniel Ek, the smart Swedish guy who founded Spotify. Or, it's Brian Chesky, Joe Gebbia, and Nathan Blecharczyk, the founders of Airbnb.

This isn't just free publicity. The stories of the great deeds of startups and their founders are harming the reputation of the established. There's always the accusatory question, "Why isn't the company we've done so much business with providing us with that new type of offering?" No wonder outsiders usually don't need to spend much on marketing. The passivity of the incumbents helps the outsiders save that money. Only after the glorifying stories of the newcomers become the talk of the day do the established begin to acknowledge the newcomers as Nightmare Competitors.

The story of the smart follower cleverly waiting for the outsiders to make a mistake, to then enter the market ends up as a myth when the newbies are given that much time. And it's not just the public and the media celebrating the apparent liberators; the capital markets play an important role, too. As we discussed earlier, investors cherish the newcomers, because they give them the chance to quickly multiply their investments. Even the best of the established can't offer comparable leverage. The stories of investors who got rich by getting in early only adds more fuel to the fire.

So, the outsiders have incredibly long lead times, a lot of glory, and all the money they need. That allows them to create economies of scale in their distinctly different business models. We've discussed in detail how Tesla is focusing on creating economies of scale in battery production and development. Ikea and Zara showed what the results are of allowing a new player to hone his logic of doing business. These once-small players were left alone far too long, and they made good use of the time, becoming stronger and stronger every year until it was too late for the established to fight them. The status of the established in the old game didn't help them succeed in the new one. Ikea and Zara are now unchallenged world market leaders in their respective fields.

Next, we'll stress why the second axis, which deals with the necessity to be bold is equally fundamental.

The established companies are usually seen as "the establishment." The naming couldn't make it clearer. And the general perception is they'll do whatever it takes to defend their privileges. But people are tired of being required to sit in run-down cabs driven by grumpy drivers. They don't want to apologize that they only want to go a few blocks. They don't want to feel guilty for not tipping generously. People are delighted when a service like Uber provides an alternative. Similarly, customers don't want to stay in sterile hotel rooms, lacking heart and soul. They don't like being charged for roaming data, and they may have good reason for losing confidence in banks. There is a hunger for bold alternatives.

The depth of this hunger was seen during the 2016 American presidential election and the "Brexit campaign in Great Britain." The negative connotation associated with "the establishment" had a decisive impact on the outcome. In this respect, lobbying to maintain the status quo needs to be seen extremely critically. It relieves pain. However, the consumption of painkillers will make any player less responsive.

Based on these two axes, the Mavericks Matrix allows us to define four quadrants. We can position all the suggestions developed in a workshop within these four quadrants.

The established, trailing the already-active Nightmare Competitor, and unable to offer superior business models are Victims. This is the position on the lower left quadrant of the matrix. Depending on the industry, the established might stay in the game with their given activities, because real or psychological barriers to switch are high. The banking industry or utilities are good examples for industries where customers are reluctant to pick providers with new business models. But these barriers are not something the players can rely upon long-term. Therefore, any suggestion that is developed in a workshop that needs to be positioned in the lower-left quadrant is obviously not what Business Model Mavericks should be striving for. The name of the quadrant was chosen to make that explicit for anybody involved in the process of creating and evaluating new business models.

MAVERICKS MATRIX

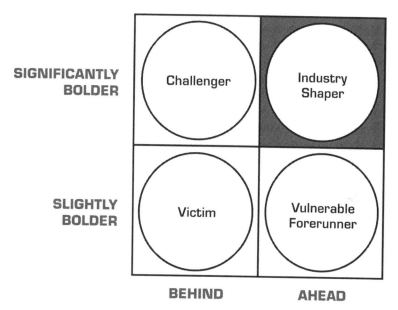

Diagram 14 *The Mavericks Matrix*

Those who offer new business models before potential Nightmare Competitors, but whose models are insufficiently bold, run the ever-present danger of being overtaken. They're what we call "Vulnerable Forerunners." The chances are high that they'll be testing the ground for those who are ready to come up with the full-blown, compromise-free business models. The name "Vulnerable Forerunner" was chosen to present an air of caution. The question, "What makes this business model vulnerable?" should be automatically asked by anybody involved in an evaluation process.

When *already* trailing, established companies need to offer business models that reach even further than those introduced by the Nightmare Competitors. If customers believe the established have avoided giving them that better offering, they will have to offer substantially more. Becoming the Nightmare Competitor of the Nightmare Competitor, for simplicity's sake, a position we've named the "Challenger" can therefore be extremely demanding.

For the reasons listed above, companies should conclude they need to be as bold and fast as possible. Only if their new business models meet these two requirements can they expect to determine the future of their industry, or as we put it, become Industry Shapers.

The Mavericks Matrix gains its power by showing that watered-down and late-launched business models are riskier than full-steam versions. The Mavericks Matrix creates a sense of urgency. Groups that work intensely on new business models in our workshops and find themselves not ideally positioned in the matrix will insist their company mustn't give anybody else the chance to determine the future of their industry. They want to occupy the market before anybody else.

If this is the outcome of a workshop, we've definitely turned managers into Business Model Mavericks. If this is the outcome, the ship is already being rocked!

Intellectually, it's no problem to follow us through the four positions of the Mavericks Matrix. And maybe you can already position your own business innovations within it. But even if you are, it might be helpful to familiarize yourself with the following examples. Unlike the examples we used to illustrate the Attacker Archetypes, these are now examples of established companies. The examples are incredibly valuable, because they make the implications of being positioned in any of the quadrants tangible for everybody. This way, further motivation to act can be generated. It's been our experience that the Mavericks Matrix, in combination with the examples, mobilize even the most reluctant delegates.

Industry Shaper

There are five examples of companies shaping or attempting to shape their industries on the basis of new customer-centric business models we'll refer to in more detail.

The first is the German steel trading company Klöckner. The company has the ambition to lead steel trading into its next orbit. The company they've founded for this purpose, kloeckner.i, provides a platform and strives to satisfy Choice Customers.

Nestle's Nespresso is a perfect example of an incumbent that has developed a new business model for Unique Value Customers.

French car manufacturer, Renault, has managed to successfully address the Bargain Customers with its Romanian daughter company, Dacia. Dacia became a Bargain Nightmare Competitor to the established.

Hilti, the renowned manufacturer of high-end drilling machines and other power tools for professionals, has introduced a new type of fleet service. On the basis of a dedicated business model, Hilti is addressing Ultimate Want Customers.

We will end with Zeppelin. It's the company founded by the German Count Zeppelin who, once upon a time, produced gigantic airships. By now, the company is one of the major distributors of Caterpillar construction machines and a big player in construction equipment rental. One of their new businesses is klickrent. This company has transferred the Airbnb business model into the world of construction equipment. They're providing new players with access to the market.

So, we'll address all Attacker Archetypes and provide three interesting B2B examples.

Klöckner & Co. is one of the world's largest steel and metal distributors. It's a truly international company employing more than 9,000 people and operating in more than fourteen countries in Europe and North America. On first view, the company appears to be a typical representative of its industry—just another conservative player in a very conservative B2B industry.

Like most players in the steel trading business, Klöckner stores enormous volumes of steel products, providing traders with a buffer between the highly inflexible steel production and customers with short-term requirements.

Klöckner alone permanently stores assets worth about $1.5 billion USD. In other words, the business is enormously capital-intensive.

Klöckner founded kloeckner.i at the end of 2014. Interestingly, the purpose of this platform is not only to digitize Klöckner's own steel trading business, it's actually open to all steel traders. The objective is to provide customers with an overview of what's available, where it's available, and the price. Furthermore, the direct connection between supply and demand becomes possible.

The advantages are easy to grasp: customers are no longer dependent on one trading partner or a limited set of such partners to get what they need. The open platform increases the chance that even the most exotic products will be available somewhere. Producers can see what's in short supply and adjust their output accordingly. The amount of assets that need to be stored can be reduced. The demand and the supply side can make use of the platform 24/7. Customers can be sure they get the best deal. It is also possible to order smaller quantities.

Klöckner is determined. The company is ready to cannibalize its own steel-trading business by allowing other traders to do business they could be taking care of. Transparency will cause margins to come under pressure. Klöckner acts on the insight that eventually, an outsider will take care of the unserved or underserved Choice Customers and become a Choice Nightmare Competitor. Klöckner has the chance to earn money for matching supply and demand on a much grander scale. They also have the chance to capitalize on associated services like transport or supply hedging.

We keep our fingers crossed that Klöckner will stay determined and not compromise. It will certainly be tough to take over and maintain the position of the Industry Shaper. Internal resistance goes without saying and direct competitors might be reluctant to strengthen the platform by participating. Some will comment sardonically on any mishap, but at the end of the day, the old guard won't be able to suppress progress.

Let's move on from Klöckner's B2B steel-trading business model to an established company that launched an enormously successful B2C business model for Unique Value Customers.

In the 1970s, the established players regarded their coffee business as a "cash cow" or "poor dog." In other words, they saw coffee at the end of its life cycle. The younger generation regarded coffee as something for senior citizens. As in most cases, it needed an outsider to change the predominant mindset. Starbucks started its business in 1971 in Seattle, and young people began to line up in front of their stores to pay a small fortune for coffee. All Starbucks did was to creatively translate and convey Italian coffee culture to an American audience.

However, there's an established player that also became an Industry Shaper: Nestlé Nespresso SA, with its globally appreciated approach to coffee drinking. Nespresso manages to sell coffee in its hermetically sealed capsules to affluent household customers at remarkably high prices. Nespresso coffee can cost upwards of $50 USD per pound. The capsules ensure the coffee aroma doesn't degrade over time, like coffee in a pack that's been opened.

Nespresso sells more than twenty different coffees and releases new editions each year. For the business market, a different system of Nespresso pods exists. Nespresso sells and licenses a number of different machines. To further deepen their customers' experience, they launched the Nespresso Club, which offers a range of exclusive and personalized customer services. Most of the capsules are ordered online or via Nespresso stores. These moves led to a turnover far north of $4 billion USD in 2016 and outstanding profitability.

However, coffee capsules and pods are becoming a commodity. Nespresso's growth has slowed from about 30 percent annually in the last decade to 7 percent in 2015. Is Nespresso systematically working on the next big industry-shaping business model, or will they share the destiny of most of the established? We hope the company that once managed to reinvent the saturated coffee market isn't going to surrender.

Let's move from Nespresso and its model to serve Unique Value Customers to the other end of the spectrum. We'll now look at an incumbent that managed to shape their industries by serving Bargain Customers.

In 1999, French car manufacturer Renault acquired the Romanian brand Dacia, which is now perfectly serving Bargain Customers. The offering consists of no-frills cars. The value-creation process is as lean as can be. Production takes place mostly in Romania, where factory and labor costs are low. Renault and its partner Nissan supply parts. Together, the companies utilize the available infrastructure and generate economies of scale. The company has a high level of integrity, as everything they do is about low price. Their marketing campaigns center around one question, "Do you still suffer from status symptoms?"

The Dacia Logan began selling at $7,850 USD in Western Europe in 2004. To this day, no other comparably sized car in the market is getting close to Dacia's pricing. Within one decade, the company was able to increase its sales by a factor of ten. Dacia now sells more than one million cars worldwide.

Famed former Volkswagen CEO Ferdinand Piech once said, "Nobody in the world needs a Dacia, people will prefer to get a secondhand VW." That was just plain wrong. It turns out that a relevant fraction of the market wants to buy a new car rather than a used one, and if that means buying a no-frills car, so be it.

We haven't yet provided any example of an established company taking care of Ultimate Want Customers in a way an incumbent could be considered an Industry Shaper. Hilti, however, is such a company. Hilti hammer drills are known by craftsmen around the world. Founded in 1941, the company is now active in more than 100 countries and employs more than 24,000 employees. Their scope of offerings expanded over the years and comprises machines for cutting, sawing, and grinding, and systems for measuring and installation, as well as consumables. Hilti is another perfect example of a company that grew on the basis of technological innovation.

Hilti figured out that others could offer similar products, and that many of the product technologies were exceeding the expectations of an increasing number of users. The rise of inexpensive battery-powered hand tools resulted in a slew of mismatched parts from a variety of manufacturers. Construction companies, consequently, faced the growing challenge of maintaining their tools over the life of a project. A broken tool, of course, can bring construction to a screeching halt. Realizing this, Hilti drew the conclusion that the *availability* of functioning equipment might be just as important as the *quality* of the equipment.

In 2006, Hilti launched its Tool Fleet Management Program. The full-service program includes a comprehensive review of a customer's current tool fleet and recommendations based on tool-usage intensity and tool age. The program doesn't require an up-front cash outlay for fleet upgrades, as the company provides one invoice per month, helping to reduce administrative costs. The program includes tool purchases, repairs, and replacement.

Hilti also added theft coverage, which can include coverage of a customer's entire tool fleet.

It's also possible to find established companies giving new players access to a market. Zeppelin has created a business model that's enlarging the market by letting companies participate that formerly weren't able to. The company is a diversified and true international player with 190 sites in thirty countries. Chairman of the Zeppelin management board, Peter Gerstmann, and his team take pride in staying true to their founder's visionary and innovative legacy.

We supported the company in rocking one of their ships: their construction rental business. The Zeppelin team followed the four steps of Customer-Centric Business Modeling and analyzed the business model of the established players in construction equipment rental. The team then identified one customer group as underserved: Choice Customers. The market was largely opaque. There was no chance to get a complete overview of what was available, where it was available, and at what price.

An even more interesting revelation was that a significant part of the market wasn't being served at all. Rental companies only purchase assets they can utilize well. An ideal product is seldom used by any single customer, but many customers need it. For each player, it's too expensive to keep as an asset, but a rental company can provide such an asset to all companies with temporary requirements.

This also explains why rental companies aren't interested in renting out highly specialized equipment that isn't needed by a substantial number of customers. Such equipment simply wouldn't be utilized properly. The big idea was to give companies who own such special equipment access to the market and thereby also attract customers that so far could not be served by rental companies.

The group came up with something that can be seen as Airbnb for construction equipment. They went back to the Business Model Radar and created a profile for a new business model. Based on that model, Zeppelin founded a new company called klickrent a few months later. klickrent provides access to the equipment of construction companies and also invites other rental companies to market *their* assets on the platform. They're enlarging availability and are offering indispensable services, such as expert assessments, maintenance, and repairs. With klickrent, Zeppelin has laid the foundation to become an Industry Shaper. It will now be difficult for other players to enter the German market with a comparable model. The more Zeppelin can keep the spirit of its mavericks alive, the longer the copy protection will last.

Examples of established companies that have become or are trying to become Industry Shapers are encouraging. Always eager to prolong our list, we ask delegates in each workshop and at each keynote address to name examples. We are sad to report the outcome is meager. Instead, we hear disillusioning background stories.

We were told, for instance, that Renault was very reluctant to sell Dacia cars in Western European markets. The company was afraid to cannibalize the sales of their Renault cars. So, they didn't sell the cars there. Instead, Dacia vehicles were successfully introduced to the Western markets via independent internationally operating dealers. After some time, Renault couldn't do anything but embrace the success.

Nespresso also seems to have stumbled into success rather than having created it systematically. George Clooney got to know the Nespresso system during a skiing vacation in Chamonix, France. He approached Nespresso and became their global ambassador. It wasn't Nespresso approaching Clooney! The Nespresso system was invented in 1970 and patented in 1976, but the Nespresso company wasn't founded until 1986, fifteen years after Starbucks.

All too often, success arrives involuntarily. Let's be more provocative. Many companies are pushed to success by sheer chance, while their strategies seem to do little or nothing to foster the success of new business models. Some business models became successful because the given systems for innovation were overruled by circumstance. As we stated in the introduction, this is the reason we feel so compelled to do something about it. There's enormous room for improvement.

Vulnerable Forerunner

The Spotify-versus-Apple case study has already shown how problematic the position of a Forerunner can be. With iTunes, Apple had the position of a Forerunner. But the company's reluctance to make use of streaming technologies made them vulnerable. Trying to safeguard its status quo business model as long as possible, Apple behaved like a typical established company.

Newspapers and special interest magazines also learned the hard way that half-hearted attempts are more of an invitation for Nightmare Competitors than progress. When the Internet took off, it became apparent that online classifieds were superior to print classifieds. However, the print media were heavily dependent on the revenues from classifieds. In the good old days, these revenues accounted for about 50 percent of the incumbents' turnover. So, they combined online ads with print ads to be able to still charge a premium. Some Nightmare Competitors were brave enough to allow private consumers to advertise for free. As a result, they received traffic, which, in turn, attracted the professionals who were willing to pay. Others followed with a freemium model or got fees for successful matching. Today, many online platforms are worth much more than their former incumbents.

Let's not forget to have a look at the industry we chose to use as a lead example: the automotive industry. Momentarily, Toyota is running into the danger of becoming a Vulnerable Forerunner.

Toyota led the market when they introduced the Prius in 1997. It was the first serious hybrid car, and despite being ridiculed for its technology and design, the car found its way. Sales grew to 1.3 million vehicles annually in 2013. Currently, a large portion of the vehicles they sell under their Toyota and Lexus brands are hybrids or can be ordered as hybrid versions. But other companies with no alternative but to become green themselves, are now catching up. Almost every car manufacturer offers hybrid options. Toyota didn't combine its technological advantage with other unique business model elements, so the others had no problem copying them. They all employ clever engineers able to creatively replicate a successful technology. And now it's Tesla that's associated with the role of environmental leader. As we discussed at length, Tesla is more of a business model innovator than a technology innovator.

But we still want to pay tribute to Toyota. Toyota is once again trying to set new standards. It introduced the Mirai to the market, the first serious attempt to establish fuel cells as a power source for vehicles. Oxygen from the air and compressed hydrogen are used as fuel for generating electricity. This electricity enables electric motors to propel cars. They're considered zero-emission vehicles as they emit only water and heat.

Toyota has teamed up with the Japanese government

in a plan to establish a full-blown charging infrastructure for hydrogen in the greater Tokyo area by 2020, when the Olympic Games will take place there. Keep in mind, the metro area is home to more than thirty-five million people. Other Japanese car manufacturers have joined in.

The magnitude of the effort required somehow explains why Toyota is inviting other players to join in. However, Toyota, as one of the biggest car manufacturers in the world, is an extremely powerful company and could have gone for "bold." The joint approach makes Toyota dependent on other parties. This leaves very little room for business model innovation. For business model innovators, it's hard to understand how Toyota missed the opportunity to substantially set itself apart.

The company still has the nimbus of being a pioneer in building green cars; it isn't dependent on problematic diesel engines like German car manufacturers. And now there's the Mirai. With respect to the Business Model Constituent "integrity," Toyota has everything it takes to make a real difference. However, they would need to get rid of the gas-guzzling Hilux and Land Cruiser. At least, it would require restricting the sales of such vehicles to areas and regions where they're actually needed.

Toyota should learn to master the discipline of business model innovation, or they'll once again be positioned in the Vulnerable Forerunner quadrant.

Even more vulnerable than Toyota are DriveNow and

car2go, the car-sharing services of BMW and Mercedes, as well as all other comparable approaches. As soon as robocabs are available in a city, their services will be largely redundant. Their only option is to be more aggressive. BMW and Mercedes seem to have realized this and are considering merging their services. We can only encourage them to be bold and fast.

Challenger and Victim

Apple is trying to fight Spotify. Whether Apple Music is going to succeed is yet to be seen. Other examples in which established companies are fighting Nightmare Competitors with a reasonable chance of success are rare. Challenging a Nightmare Competitor is much more difficult than being a Forerunner. A Forerunner requires only a technological innovation, while becoming a Nightmare Competitor Challenger requires the scarce ability to create business models.

So far, the established all too often end up as victims. There's a saying in the military that the defenders are often in a pitiful position. They realize they'll run out of food while fortified in their castles. Already weakened, they have no choice but to leave their stronghold to meet their waiting attacker. In the same way, the once-proud established often become oppressed by the ones they previously ridiculed.

Lufthansa is an example of an established airline that's trying to challenge the attack from Ryanair. The retaliation thus far, however, has been far from perfect.

The German company was once renowned for great strategic moves. Lufthansa was one of the founding members of Star Alliance. The "Miles and More" program was introduced in 1993 and was one of the first frequent traveler programs in Europe. Lufthansa also founded Sky Chefs, Lufthansa Technik, Lufthansa Consulting, Lufthansa Systems, and Global Load Control, companies serving the entire industry. This allowed Lufthansa to generate economies of scale while keeping crucial parts of the value-creation system under control. However, Lufthansa was not at all prepared when the budget airlines started to interfere. Ryanair started its operations in 1984. Southwest even earlier, in 1967.

In response, Lufthansa finally introduced their low-cost airline, Germanwings in 2002. Today, their budget activities are consolidated under the name "Eurowings." But regardless of the name, Lufthansa's budget approach does not really follow the Bargain Nightmare Competitor rulebook. It relies on the major airports. Therefore, they pay much more for takeoffs and landings than their nightmarish rivals. Fewer flights are on time because there's more traffic at major airports, and planes often have to wait for connecting flights. Different types of aircrafts are used, it's possible to collect miles, and many of the inclusive services, especially ground services like lounges are offered, too. In terms of marketing, Eurowings follows the role model of Lufthansa.

Are Lufthansa's customers delighted? Not really. Lufthansa doesn't give customers a choice anymore. Eurowings provides short-to-medium, point-to-point routes in Europe, paying specific attention to the group's home markets, namely, Germany, Austria, Switzerland, and Belgium. Long-haul routes that still rely on the hub system are served by Lufthansa. Even in the days of Germanwings, where customers sometimes had the chance to take either a Germanwings or a Lufthansa plane, the price was clearly influenced by what marketing calls "harvesting." It's the science of extracting as much from a given customer as possible. Offering the best fares in the industry was clearly never the main objective.

Today, even employees are as confused by name changes and new policies as customers are. Taking into account their highly interdependent system of current and new business, it's easy to explain why the airline has been paralyzed by strikes. It isn't clear to most employees why some are still entitled to enormous privileges while others are deprived of them.

Lufthansa is still one of the best traditional airlines. For the first two quarters of 2017, the company announced record profits, and the budget activities are slowly reaching profitability. However, from a strategic perspective, they are still vulnerable. And imagine what strategic and financial position the airline could be in if their budget activities, and not Ryanair, had been highly profitable over so many years.

A similar story of a failing attempt to attack a Nightmare Competitor is observable in the strategy BMW is pursuing with BMWi to fight Tesla. BMW is one of the world's top car brands. No other player is as good at detecting ever-new niches. With the Mini brand, they showed the world that small cars can be premium. Their production processes are highly flexible and efficient. Among all established car manufacturers, BMW is regarded as one of the most forward-thinking companies. To the astonishment of many rivals, they launched BMWi in 2011. The mission of this sub-brand is to design and manufacture plug-in electric vehicles. Serial production of the BMW i3 began in September 2013. The even more futuristic-looking BMW i8 was launched in June 2014.

This all sounds progressive, but let's not compare BMW's efforts with those of other established players. As soon as we compare BMW's efforts with Tesla, a far less flattering story unfolds. As you're by now aware, Tesla was founded in 2003 and gained widespread attention with the launch of its Roadster in 2008. The company's second vehicle, the Model S, debuted in 2012. BMW was not as late as Lufthansa but late nevertheless. The Nightmare Competitor had been allowed the opportunity of setting the standards.

While the BMWi models are green, the BMW organization can hardly be seen as an environmental leader when you consider their wide range of conventional vehicles. Unlike Tesla, having their own infrastructure of charging stations wasn't an option, and neither was free charging, even over a short span of time. The cars are sold through the same BMW sales network. And the same old means of marketing are as important as ever. The campaign accompanying the launch of the "i" models was massive. Unlike Tesla, BMW isn't focused in any way on developing economies of scale in the most expensive element of electro-mobility, the battery. In short, BMW is selling a new range of products—electric cars—in the established system.

Once again, we can observe a company entangled in compromises. The old guard within the company is mockingly referring to the disappointing sales success. In their opinion, BMW should stay true to its combustion engine-related brand heritage. BMW was also one of the frontrunners when the German car manufacturers lobbied for governmental incentives for electric vehicles. This isn't how opinion leaders are positioning themselves.

In Chapter 4, we showed how to make practical use of the insights and methods provided in Chapters 1 to 3. By running Rocking the Ship Workshops, companies are able to collectively develop new Customer-Centric Business Models ahead of potential Nightmare Competitors. There will be readers who say, "That's all I wanted," and they might want to follow it up right away. Of course, that's fine with us.

But what happens after new ideas are created? They need to be placed within the context of the current business.

After all, we've written this book with the established organizations in mind. In Chapter 5, we'll therefore venture into the realm of implementation. We'll introduce strategies that allow organizations to embrace the unorthodox business models that typically are required to define the future of industries.

⑤

KEEP ON ROCKING

Let's assume you've created a monster. You nailed it in your Rocking the Ship Workshop. You conveyed to your colleagues the power that can unfold from playfully and virtually creating Nightmare Competitors. You applied Customer-Centric Business Modeling and came up with great new business models. By using the Mavericks Matrix to assess all your suggestions, you were able to identify the business model with the greatest potential to ultimately rock your industry. Despite these successes, however, you feel uncomfortable. Or maybe you feel uncomfortable *because* of these successes. In all probability, the nightmarish approach contradicts everything your company has done thus far. The virtual Nightmare Competitor is indeed monstrous.

In following our recommendation, you invited a broad spectrum of managers into the workshop. People from a variety of departments have participated. Everyone shares the feeling of excitement mixed with unease. Everyone is asking the same question, "Will we be able to convince the rest of the organization to put this new idea in practice?"

The managers who represented the marketing department in the workshop are uncomfortable, because they know their colleagues will have a problem with the new business. They will raise concerns that the new approach isn't compatible with what the company's brand stands for. Naming the new business differently could be seen as an option, but they'll still fear that customers would nevertheless associate the new business with the established company.

The managers who represented sales in the workshop are even more uncomfortable. They are afraid their colleagues will do whatever they can to avoid the new approach. Their peers will struggle with the fact that the new business could cannibalize the given offering. They see their bonuses in danger.

The finance managers might be concerned because they fear the margins will be reduced, or because more assets will be needed. The managers in production could be caught off guard because other capabilities are required. You won't have any problem extending the list of colleagues who have not participated in the workshop but are likely to be irritated as soon as they learn the results. The new won't have many friends in the established organization.

You really can't blame these managers, can you? They've been tasked with taking care of synergies for as long as they have been onboard the spaceship. When the company acquired a new business activity, it was always a similar spaceship, and they had to align it to increase economies of scale. It's only natural they use the established business as a yardstick with which to evaluate any additional business. But given this approach, radically new activities are likely to be dismissed. If they aren't dismissed, they'll fall victim to untold compromises. This turns any new approach into something that's a mere shadow of the original concept and will come crashing back down shortly after launch. The conservative-minded will see this faltering as confirmation: "We should never have started it. I should have been even more critical," they might say.

There's only one way to avoid this situation: keep the new business separate and go for it. And if you personally can't make this decision, you should convey the following message to the ones who do:

There is the current business. It's the business that generates the turnover and the profits we're all dependent upon today. We'd be foolhardy to question that business as long as enough customers continue to appreciate it. Full stop."

But there are customers who aren't completely happy with what we and our competitors, in short, what the industry is providing. That means we will lose these customers as soon as Nightmare Competitors launch business models better meeting their requirements. Our company needs to occupy the space before they can. This will not only compensate for losses in the traditional business, but it will also allow us to take businesses away from other established companies. The new business is the sharpest weapon with which to fight our direct rivals. It's a weapon they don't know how to handle. We'll be able to tell an awesome growth story when we get it right. But for this to happen, the new business needs to be managed in its own right and without interference. Full stop.

When top management has invited you to run the workshop and has made itself familiar with the method in advance, just as we discussed in Chapter 4, you will not have much headwind anyhow. The impatient and ambitious top managers, in particular, should be in Angel's Advocate mode, and rather than object to your reasoning, should question whether you're being extreme enough.

If you decide to run radically new businesses separately, the established one is no longer the yardstick for the new. New and established businesses can be run on their own terms, allowing the following beautiful story to possibly unfold.

Having multiple options, customers can decide for themselves what approach they like and when it's the right time to make use of alternatives. No matter what customers ultimately decide, the company will win. Since the company is allowing its customers to choose, traditional strategic planning loses importance. Resources are simply allocated based on the market success of each business model.

By providing a home for multiple businesses, the traditional concept of change also loses importance. It's no longer necessary to align all employees in following one predefined new direction. As in any organization, there are first movers, who, freed from their shackles, can show what they envisioned can, indeed, be done. They get easy access to resources to build their spacecraft and put their ideas into practice. With this, they have the chance to create the proof of concept that might lead the more conservative employees to reconsider their position.

These more conservative employees will then apply for jobs with the new businesses when they're ready. The internal transformation process can be in tune with the change in customers' preferences. Best-case scenario, this happens without hard feelings, outplacement programs, and so on.

When a company becomes home to a broad number of heterogeneous businesses, it is following what we call a "Habitat Strategy."

There are mavericks who see a necessity of going even beyond the Habitat Strategy. They don't question that the businesses should be kept separate. However, they ask if the established business couldn't help the new businesses by providing even better preconditions to succeed. It's from this shifted perspective of the new business that they look at the established business.

Klöckner and Zeppelin provide role models for this change in perspective. The traditional steel-trading business of Klöckner is the major supplier to the independent kloeckner.i steel-trading platform. By being provided with this input, kloeckner.i can overcome the great challenge of all platforms: to offer enough interesting content right from the start.

klickrent benefits from the input of Zeppelin in the same way. Zeppelin's traditional rental business is giving its independent digital platform access to construction equipment as basic content. The additional content provided by the construction companies renting out their equipment complements the equipment provided by Zeppelin Rental. And by giving competing rental companies access to the platform, Zeppelin enlarges the basis for offering maintenance work, forwarding, expert assessments, and so on even further.

Any company active in an industry where there is no Choice Nightmare Competitor should consider founding such a platform providing choice. Like Klöckner and Zeppelin, they might be able to leverage the content their established business can provide. The more content, the greater the advantage the new business can gain. This way, the company can make sure not to become dependent on a third-party that establishes itself as a gatekeeper to its industry.

Is the logic of putting the new business first also applicable for business models designed to serve other types of customers? The Renault and Dacia case already showed that established entities can support new entities in satisfying Bargain Customers. Dacia is in a favorable position to take care of these customers, because the Renault car company and its partner company, Nissan, are suppliers to Dacia. For Dacia, it would be impossible to come up with the economies of scale the much bigger companies, Nissan and Renault, can create. This allows Dacia to further reduce costs and be extremely aggressive with pricing.

In the beginning, Unique Value Customers are often ready to forgive a product and service lacking in performance. Tesla's production quality is regarded by experts as inferior to what the incumbents offer. The iPhone in its original version was a lousy phone: the camera wasn't the best available, the Edge standard for data transmission offered only slow Internet access. Even the most enthusiastic fans aren't willing to accept such shortcomings for very long. Imagine the power that could be unleashed by a new entity with the liberty to introduce something so dramatically different than a Tesla car or an iPhone, and at the same time, had unhindered access to crucial competences and assets of the established. And for business models designed to serve Access Customers, the same is of course true.

When the new is unconditionally supported by the established, we call this a "Booster Strategy."

The Booster Strategy is more difficult to implement. For proud established businesses with many employees and in charge of most of the company's turnover and profits, it is quite a step to support much smaller, new entities. This support can be in conflict with their own interests. When it comes to supporting choice offerings, you need to have transparency, which will intensify competition. And most other new activities will be seen as direct rivals. Those activities specifically addressing Unique Value, Bargain, and Ultimate Want Customers will reduce the number of customers still interested in the traditional offering. So why should the established provide assistance in making the new activities successful?

Sometimes it's essential to apply the Booster Strategy to even have a chance of success. You need it when you're facing Nightmare Competitors that are also bringing their own boosters into the game. In our case studies, we've referred in detail to Amazon and Google. They shed their startup status quite some time ago and are now industry outsiders with the advantage that they can leverage the competencies and assets out of their home industries to turn other industries upside down. This, along with the financial power they've obtained, make them enormously dangerous for any established industry player.

Even the proudest of established businesses should strive to strengthen new business activities launched in their corporate context rather than either becoming a supplier to the most dangerous Nightmare Competitors or being crushed by them. The Nightmare Competitors have the power to deprive them of all their dignity. And it must be assumed they will make use of their power. In contrast, the Booster Strategy also provides all the same opportunities for internal transformation that the Habitat Strategy offers.

We're aware we've gone to some extremes with our examples. But what choice do you have when the whole story is about extreme thinking? There are certainly cases in which compromises are sensible or even positive for the established and the new businesses. Between black and white, there are always shades of grey. But whenever we see grey, we become suspicious, e.g., when Dacia cars are sold by Renault dealers, we wonder whether the reflex to create synergies has simply gained the upper hand again.

And even though we positioned Hilti, with its fleet service as an industry-shaping company in the Mavericks Matrix, we're not sure whether they'll remain unchallenged. The fleet service is based on a specific business model. It has its specific value-creation system, a specific model for utilization, and a specific revenue model. So far, so good. However, the fleet service bears the Hilti brand name and is advertised on the website alongside the traditional business. It would be extremely hard for an alternatively named new business entity to establish a comparable reputation like Hilti and ramp up its own sales activities. But, that said, mingling the two businesses makes the new business completely dependent on the established business. There's no chance to look for another sales partner when sales prefer instead to sell the traditional products. And we wonder whether Hilti's fleet management sufficiently takes care of customers who also appreciate other brands.

So, instead of opening up to shades of grey and compromises, we would like to encourage all those who start to acknowledge that what they learned in the old days, when the spaceships were unchallenged and when synergies were the Holy Grail, doesn't necessarily work anymore. And we're delighted to see that more and more companies actively search for new methods and approaches. Not all managers of corporate functions defend their turf in the manner we described at the beginning of this chapter.

There are human resource departments which understand that turnover, profit, and headcount are insufficient criteria for assessing the contribution a manager provides to the company's success. These criteria are, of course, favorable to those in charge of the established business. But incentives also need to be provided for those willing to start small and to take risks to lead the company into the future. If companies truly want to support internal entrepreneurship, they need to back that idea up. So, to reduce the potential pain of managers charged with boosting the new business, the HR departments experiment with variable compensations based on the overall and long-term performance of the company rather than the traditional compensation models.

There are legal departments which understand that protecting the organization from potential risk isn't the only job they should take care of. Amazon employed the best lawyers in the world to make 1-click possible. It's in that same spirit that these legal departments try to find ways to offer progressive solutions to their internal clients.

There are IT departments which understand that different businesses have different requirements. They ask for the tools they want to use, the safety standards they see as adequate, the response time they require, the price points they can accept, and so on.

There are financial departments which understand that the same set of performance criteria can't be used to measure very diverse businesses. They see it as their task to develop specific performance criteria for the different businesses. In this context, they also question paradigms like the ones which say, "We only invest in business cases that show a return on investment within three years." They're aware that everyone knows to tweak the assumptions to meet the goal, and that some businesses that might be crucial for the future of the company can't be pursued due to such self-imposed standards.

There are investor relations departments which understand that it's up to them to attract investors who are not driven by dividends alone. They try to learn from the many firms out there showing their investors how their great ideas to define the future of the industry boost stock prices. And they are able to explain that such increases in stock prices are usually much more attractive than dividends.

The progressive managers of these and other departments also acknowledge that they need to let go of the reins. It's a precondition for the diverse businesses to be as autonomous as required. And so, they take pleasure in coaching the businesses and developing new tools with which to propel the whole organization into the next orbit.

Such companies will attract the crazy ones, the round pegs in the square holes, the ones who see things differently. Employing the best of them aboard their spaceships, their spacecrafts, and in their ground control stations, these companies will keep on rocking.

89954946R00115

Made in the USA
Middletown, DE
19 September 2018